A reason for Science
Hands-On Activities with Scripture Values

LEVEL A

STUDENT WORKTEXT

ISBN #1-58938-207-2

Published by The Concerned Group, Inc.
700 East Granite • PO Box 1000 • Siloam Springs, AR 72761

Authors	**Dave & Rozann Seela**
Publisher	**Russ L. Potter, II**
Senior Editor	**Bill Morelan**
Project Coordinator	**Rocki Vanatta**
Guided Reading Consultant	**Susan Hancock**
Creative Director	**Daniel Potter**
Proofreaders	**Tricia S. Williams & Lou Stewart**
Step Illustrations	**Josh Ray & Steven Butler**
Character Illustrations	**Josh Ray**
Colorists	**Josh & Aimee Ray**

Printed on recycled paper in the United States

For more information about A Reason For® curricula,
write to the address above, call, or visit our website.

www.AReasonFor.com
800.447.4332

Dear Parent,

Welcome to a new school year! This letter is to introduce you to **A Reason For**© Science.

A Reason For© Science teaches basic Life, Earth, and Physical Science through a unique combination of direct instruction and fun, hands-on activities. Each lesson is tied directly to the **National Science Education Standards** and uses an inquiry-based approach designed to enhance learning.

Today's increasingly complex world requires a clear understanding of science and technology. Our future prosperity depends on helping children rediscover the challenges, excitement, and joy of science (especially in the context of Scripture values). Thus, one of the primary goals of **A Reason For**© Science is to make science not only meaningful, but also FUN!

Fun, Flexible Format

Instead of a hardback textbook filled with "facts" to memorize, your child will be working in an interactive worktext that helps develop critical-thinking skills. Students start each week with an overview designed to engage their interest. This is followed by a direct instruction component in the form of a story. (Options are provided to meet the needs of Emergent, Transitional, and Fluent readers.) A weekly hands-on activity focuses on one key science concept, followed by group discussion and thought-provoking questions. Lessons conclude with various assessments to verify students' mastery of the key concept.

Safety Issues

The hands-on nature of **A Reason For**© Science means your child will be working with age-appropriate materials. (For instance, the "acids" the teacher uses are actually diluted forms comparable to typical household chemicals.) Like a field trip or gym class, science activities require simple safety precautions. But for instructional reasons, all materials in **A Reason For**© Science are treated as hazardous. This encourages students to develop good safety habits for use in later years.

Scripture Values

Best of all, **A Reason For**© Science features Scripture values! Every lesson concludes with a Scripture object lesson related to the week's topic. As the teacher shares this "Food for Thought," students can relate the week's lesson to a Scriptural theme, providing a positive way to integrate faith and learning.

Here's to an exciting year exploring God's world!

Dave & Rozann Seela
Authors, **A Reason For**© Science

EXPLORING GOD'S WORLD! Science

A Reason For© Science makes science FUN! It's filled with hands-on activities, colorful discovery sheets, and lots of discussion and exploration. This year you'll discover many exciting new things as you explore God's world!

Although "almost everything relates to everything else" in some way or another, scientists usually divide science into three broad areas for study: **Life Science**, **Earth Science**, and **Physical Science**. The sections in your worktext are based on these categories.

Colorful icons are used to help you identify each section. An **ant** represents **Life Science** lessons. A **globe** stands for **Earth Science** lessons. An **atom** (energy/matter) or a **hammer** (forces) is used to introduce **Physical Science** lessons.

Life Science

Life Science is the study of **living things.** In the Life Science section of your **A Reason For©** Science worktext, you'll explore different kinds of living things. You'll learn about their characteristics (how they are alike or different). You'll discover how scientists classify (label and sort) living things. You'll even learn about life cycles and how they work!

Earth Science

Earth Science is the study of **earth** and **sky**. In the Earth Science section of your **A Reason For©** Science worktext, you'll explore the structure of our planet (rocks, fossils), and patterns of change on Earth (days, nights, months, years). We'll even take a look at the solar system, and what causes an eclipse.

Physical Science

Physical Science is the study of **energy**, **matter**, and related **forces**. Since physical science has a big effect on our daily lives, we'll spend more time on this section. Here are the two areas we'll focus on:

Energy and Matter

Whenever you see the "atom girl" in your **A Reason For**© Science worktext, you'll learn about the different **states** and unique **properties** of **matter**. You'll discover new things about light and sound. You'll explore physical and chemical reactions. You'll also find out more about electicity and magnetism.

Forces

Lessons that start with the "little hammer" focus on forces. You'll discover how "**push** and **pull**" form the basis for all physical movement. You'll explore simple machines (levers, pulleys). You'll work with Newton's laws of motion. You'll even learn to understand concepts like torque, inertia, and buoyancy.

Safety First!

Before you begin, be sure you meet "Peat" the safety worm (see next page). Peat's job is to warn you if there's a potential hazard. Whenever you see Peat and his warning sign, be sure to **STOP** and wait for further instructions from your teacher!

Exploring God's world of science often requires using equipment or materials that can injure you if they're not handled correctly. Also, many accidents occur simply because people are in a hurry, are careless, or ignore safety rules.

It's your responsibility to know and observe the rules and to use care and caution as you work. Just like when you're on the playground, horseplay or ignoring safety rules can be dangerous. Don't let an accident happen to you!

Meet "Peat" the Safety Worm!

Peat's job is to warn you whenever there's a potential hazard around. Whenever you see Peat and his warning sign, **STOP** and wait for further instructions from your teacher!

Peat's sign helps you know what kind of hazard is present. Before beginning each activity, your teacher will discuss this hazard in detail and review any special safety rules that apply to that activity.

means this activity requires **PROTECTIVE GEAR.**

Usually **gloves** or **goggles** (or both) are required. Goggles protect your eyes from things like flying debris or splashing liquids. Gloves protect your hands from things like heat, broken glass, or corrosive chemicals.

means there is a **BURN HAZARD.** There are three common burn hazards.

Open Flame indicates the presence of fire (often matches or a candle). Thermal Burn means objects may be too hot to touch. Corrosion indicates a chemical substance is present.

means there is a **POISON HAZARD.**

There are three common poison hazards. Skin Contact indicates a substance that should not touch skin. Vapor indicates fumes that should not be inhaled. Hygiene indicates the presence of materials that may contain germs.

indicates OTHER HAZARDS.

There are three additional hazards that require caution. Breakage indicates the presence of fragile substances (like glass). Slipping indicates liquids that might spill on the floor, making it slippery. Sharp Objects indicates the presence of tools with sharp edges or points.

Play It Safe!

Exploring God's world with **A Reason For** Science can be great fun, but remember — play it safe! Be sure you observe all the safety rules. Handle equipment and materials carefully, and always remember to stay cautious and alert.

And don't forget Peat the Safety Worm! Whenever you see Peat and his warning sign, **STOP** and wait for further instructions from your teacher.

Life Science

Life Science is the study of **living things.** In this section, you'll explore different kinds of living things. You'll learn their characteristics (how they are alike or different). You'll discover how scientists classify (label and sort) living things. You'll even learn about life cycles and how they work!

FOCUS Basic Needs

OBJECTIVE To explore some basic needs of plants and animals

OVERVIEW Plants and animals need certain things in order to "survive and thrive." Some of the most important needs are food, water, air, and sunlight.

WHAT TO DO

With your team, carefully follow each step below.

Observe

Look at the two plants your teacher gives you. **Look** at the soil they are planted in. **Look** at their leaves. **Think** about what these plants might need to live.

Describe

Describe the two plants. What **color** are they? What **shape** are the leaves? In what ways are the two plants the same? In what ways are they different?

Discuss

Name one thing a plant might need to live. food

Name another thing a plant might need. water

What else might plants need to live? sunlight

Plants and animals need certain things to survive. Some of these include **food**, **water**, **air**, and **sunlight**. Read the story below to find out more.

Basic Needs

Plants and animals have needs.

Plants and animals need certain things in order to survive. Some of these needs are food, water, air, and sunlight. If its needs are not met, a plant or animal could die.

Food and water are needs.

Plants and animals need water.

All plants need water. Without it, they dry up and die. Animals need water, too. Most can only live a few days without water.

Plants and animals need food.

Plants get food (nutrients) from the soil. They also make food from sunlight (photosynthesis). Animals get food from plants and sometimes other animals.

Air and sunlight are needs.

Plants and animals need air.

Plants use air in a different way than animals, but both need air to survive. Without air, an animal would die in minutes.

Plants and animals need sunlight.

When animals "soak up sun," it builds Vitamin D in their bodies. When plants use sunlight, they use it to make food.

Needs can be different.

Every kind of plant has special needs.

A cactus needs lots of sun, but little water. A fern needs lots of water, but little sun. Different places support different plants.

Every kind of animal has special needs.

A beaver can't live in a desert. A camel can't live in a swamp. Like plants, animals only survive where their needs can be met.

WHAT I LEARNED - part 1

Discuss the story with your team, then answer the questions below.

1 Name four basic needs that plants and animals have.

_____

_____

_____

_____

_____

2 How are a cactus' needs like a fern's? How are they different?

_____

_____

_____

_____

_____

_____

3 What might happen to a tree frog in the desert? Why?

_____

_____

_____

_____

_____

DO THE ACTIVITY

Working with your research team, carefully follow each step below. Before you start, be sure you know the **safety rules** for this activity.

STEP 1

Place Plant 1 in a sunny location. **Water** it as your teacher directs. (This plant is the "control" for the experiment. A control is a standard for comparing things.)

STEP 2

Take Plant 2 out of its container. **Remove** the soil from the roots. **Seal** Plant 2 in a plastic bag, then **watch** as your teacher seals all the bags in a box.

STEP 3

Wait three days. **Remove** Plant 2 from the box and **compare** it with Plant 1 (the control). **Talk** about differences between the two plants.

STEP 4

Review each step. **Discuss** what needs Plant 2 had that were not being met. **Compare** your observations with those of other research teams.

WHAT I LEARNED - part 2

Discuss the activity with your team, then answer the questions below.

1 What needs did Plant 2 have that were not being met?

_____

_____

_____

_____

_____

_____

2 After step 3, how was Plant 2 different from Plant 1?

_____

_____

_____

_____

_____

_____

3 If you moved a flower into a cave, what might happen? Why?

_____

_____

_____

_____

_____

_____

SHOW WHAT YOU KNOW - 1

Plants and animals need certain things to survive.
Some of these include **food**, **water**, **air**, and **sunlight**.
Circle the pictures below that show basic needs.

The basic needs of plants and animals include what four things?

_____

- -

To the Parent . . . **Scripture Connection:** Philippians 4:19

Lesson Focus:
Basic Needs

Lesson Objective:
To explore some basic needs of plants and animals

National Science Education Standards:
Standard C1 — *"All students should develop an understanding of the characteristics of organisms . . . Organisms have basic needs. . . Organisms can survive only in environments in which their needs can be met . . ."*

Follow-up Questions:
Ask your child to describe some basic needs of plants and animals (food, water, air, sunlight).
Ask your child to explain what happens when needs are not being met (the plant or animal may die).
Ask your child to explain how needs may differ (a cactus needs lots of sun, but little water — a fern is the opposite; etc.).

FOCUS Plant Structure and Function

OBJECTIVE To explore structure and function by studying the parts of plants

OVERVIEW Every part of a plant is made in a certain way (structure) so that it can do a certain kind of job (function). All the parts must work together to keep the plant healthy and alive.

WHAT TO DO

With your team, carefully follow each step below.

Observe

Look at your plant. **Look** at its leaves. **Look** at its stem. **Move** some dirt away and **look** at the plant's roots.

Describe

Describe the leaves, the stem, and the roots. What do they **look** like? What do they **smell** like? What do they **feel** like?

Discuss

What part of a plant is usually at the top? leaves

What part is usually in the middle? stems

What part usually grows underground? roots

READ THE STORY

The three main parts of a plant are the **roots**, the **stem**, and the **leaves**. Read the story below to find out how they work together to keep the plant alive.

Plant Parts

Plants have many parts. All the parts help the plant.

Every part of a plant is made in a certain way (structure) so that it can do a certain kind of job (function). All the parts work together to keep the plant alive.

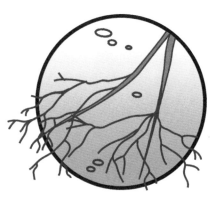

These are roots.

Plants have roots.

A plant's roots grow underground. They spread in all directions. The larger the plant, the farther the root system spreads.

The roots help feed the plant.

Roots keep the plant in place and hold the soil around it. Roots also absorb water and nutrients from the soil.

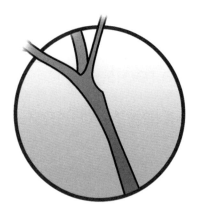

These are stems.

Plants have stems.

A plant's stem connects the roots to the leaves. A tree trunk is a very large plant stem.

The stem helps support the plant.

The stem supports the plant. It also carries water and nutrients from the roots to other parts of the plant.

These are leaves.

Plants have leaves.

Leaves come in many sizes and shapes. Leaves direct water to the roots and help keep rain from washing the soil away.

The leaves help protect the plant.

Leaves also absorb sunshine, turning it into food for the plant. Plants are the only living things that make their own food.

WHAT I LEARNED - part 1

Discuss the story with your team, then answer the questions below.

1 What do the roots do to help the plant?

_____

_____

_____

_____

_____

_____

2 What does the stem do to help the plant?

_____

_____

_____

_____

_____

_____

3 What do the leaves do to help the plant?

_____

_____

_____

_____

_____

DO THE ACTIVITY

Working with your research team, carefully follow each step below. Before you start, be sure you know the **safety rules** for this activity.

STEP 1

Sit on a chair with your hands in your lap. **Ask** a team member to **push** you sideways gently. How hard is it to stay on the chair? Trade places and **repeat** until everyone has had a turn.

STEP 2

Sit on the chair again. **Hold** it with your hands and feet. **Ask** a team member to gently **push** you sideways. How hard is it to stay on the chair? Why? **Repeat** until everyone has had a turn.

STEP 3

Fill a cup half full of water. **Watch** as your teacher adds food coloring. (This represents the food that a plant needs.) Now **cut** a paper towel into strips an inch wide.

STEP 4

Carefully **dip** the strip in the water. **Observe** what happens. Now **discuss** each step, then **compare** your observations with other research teams.

WHAT I LEARNED - part 2

Discuss the activity with your team, then answer the questions below.

1 What plant parts does this activity represent? How?

_____

_____

_____

_____

_____

_____

_____

2 How are roots and stems alike? How are they different?

_____

_____

_____

_____

_____

_____

_____

3 If a plant lost all its roots, what might happen? Why?

_____

_____

_____

_____

_____

_____

SHOW WHAT YOU KNOW - 1

Color the **leaves** of the plant green. Color the **stem** of the plant brown. Color the **roots** of the plant red. Write the name of each plant part below.

These are the

_____

_ _ _ _ _ _ _ _ _ _

_____

This is the

_____

_ _ _ _ _ _ _ _ _ _

_____

These are the

_____

_ _ _ _ _ _ _ _ _ _

_____

To the Parent . . .   **Scripture Connection:** Genesis 1:11-12

Lesson Focus:
Plant Structure and Function

Lesson Objective:
To discover that plant parts are made in a certain way (structure) to do specific jobs (function)

National Science Education Standards:
Standard C1 — *"All students should develop an understanding of the characteristics of organisms . . .*
Each plant or animal has different structures that serve different functions . . ."

Follow-up Questions:
Ask your child to describe roots, then explain one thing they do (roots hold plants in place; absorb water/nutrients).
Ask your child to describe a plant's stem, then explain one thing it does (stem connect roots to leaves; supports plant).
Ask your child to describe a plant's leaves, then explain one thing they do (leaves absorb sunlight; help plant make food).

FOCUS Animal Structure and Function

OBJECTIVE To explore structure and function by studying what animals "wear"

OVERVIEW Different creatures have different kinds of coverings (structure). These different coverings do different jobs (function). A creature's covering helps keep it healthy and alive.

WHAT TO DO

With your team, carefully follow each step below.

Observe

Look carefully at the three animal coverings.

Look at the **fur**. Look at the **feathers**.

Look at the **scales**.

Describe

Describe the **fur**, the **feathers**, and the **scales**.

What do they **look** like? What do they **smell** like?

What do they **feel** like?

Discuss

What covering might a bear have? fur

What covering might a bird have? feathers

What covering might a fish have? scales

Some animals have **fur**. Some have **feathers**. Some have **scales**. Read the story below to find out how different coverings help different animals.

Animal Parts

Different kinds of animals have different coverings.

Every covering is made in a certain way (structure) so that it can do a certain kind of job (function). An animal's covering helps keep it healthy and alive.

This is fur.

Some animals have fur.

Fur is a thick layer of hair. Mammals have fur. There are many kinds of mammals — from tiny mice to huge bears.

Fur keeps mammals warm.

Fur helps keep mammals warm in very cold places. Without its warm layer of fur, a mammal would die.

This is a feather.

Some animals have feathers.

Birds have feathers. There are many different kinds of birds — from the tiny hummingbird to the huge ostrich.

Feathers keep birds dry.

Feathers are covered with a special oil that helps them shed water. Without its feathers, a bird would die.

This is a scale.

Some animals have scales.

Fish have scales. There are many different kinds of fish — from tiny goldfish to huge sailfish.

Scales help fish swim.

Scales make the body of the fish very smooth. This helps the fish swim very fast. Without its scales, a fish would die.

WHAT I LEARNED - part 1

Discuss the story with your team, then answer the questions below.

1 Name an animal with fur. How does fur help this animal?

_____

_____

_____

_____

_____

2 Name an animal with feathers. How do feathers help this animal?

_____

_____

_____

_____

_____

3 Name an animal with scales. How do scales help this animal?

_____

_____

_____

_____

_____

DO THE ACTIVITY

Working with your research team, carefully follow each step below. Before you start, be sure you know the **safety rules** for this activity.

STEP 1

Blow on your hand. **Describe** how cool it feels. **Place** the fur on your hand, then **blow** on it. How does this feel? **Discuss** how fur might keep an animal warm.

STEP 2

Dip a cotton ball in water, then try to **blow** it dry. **Repeat** using a feather. **Compare** the results. **Discuss** how feathers might help keep a bird dry.

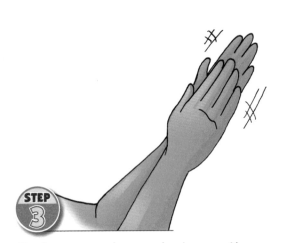

STEP 3

Rub your hands together rapidly. **Feel** the warmth. **Wet** your palms and **repeat**. How does this feel? Scales reduce friction. **Discuss** how this helps a fish.

STEP 4

Now **review** each step in this activity. **Discuss** how each kind of covering helps the creature. **Compare** your observations with other research teams.

WHAT I LEARNED - part 2

Discuss the activity with your team, then answer the questions below.

1 Why do ducks have feathers? Why don't they have fur?

2 How are fur, feathers, and scales alike? How are they different?

3 If a polar bear lost all its fur, what might happen? Why?

SHOW WHAT YOU KNOW - 1

Circle the **mammals** in brown. Circle the **birds** in yellow. Circle the **fish** in green. Now complete each sentence to tell what kind of covering each animal has.

_____

___ ___ ___ ___ ___

are covered with feathers.

_____

___ ___ ___ ___ ___

are covered with fur.

_____

___ ___ ___ ___ ___

are covered with scales.

To the Parent . . .   **Scripture Connection:** Genesis 1:20-25

Lesson Focus:
Animal Structure and Function

Lesson Objective:
To discover that animal coverings are made in a certain way (structure) to do specific jobs (function)

National Science Education Standards:
Standard C1 — *"All students should develop an understanding of the characteristics of organisms . . .*
Each plant or animal has different structures that serve different functions . . ."

Follow-up Questions:
Ask your child to describe fur, then explain how fur helps mammals (fur can help keep an animal warm).
Ask your child to describe feathers, then explain how feathers help birds (feathers help keep birds dry).
Ask your child to describe scales, then explain how scales help fish (scales make a fish smooth, helping it swim faster).

Lively Larva
Lesson 4

FOCUS   Life Cycles (larva)

OBJECTIVE   To explore the larva stage of a moth's life cycle

OVERVIEW   Moth eggs (stage 1) hatch into larva (stage 2) that are called caterpillars. Caterpillars eat almost constantly to get energy for the pupa (stage 3) part of their life cycle.

WHAT TO DO

With your team, carefully follow each step below.

Observe

Think about a caterpillar you have seen (in nature, books, or on TV). How did it move around? How was it like other caterpillars? How was it different?

Describe

Describe another caterpillar you have seen. What did it **look** like? What color was it? What shape was it? What do you think it would **feel** like?

Discuss

How do you think caterpillars get around? crawl

What do caterpillars do most of the time? eat

What do you think caterpillars like to eat? leaves

A **caterpillar** is actually just one step in the life cycle of a **moth**. Read the story below to find out more about this stage of the moth's life.

Caterpillars

A caterpillar is one stage in a moth's life.

Insects often change into different forms as they grow. Scientists call this a life cycle. Moths go through four stages: egg, larva, pupa, and adult. Then the cycle repeats.

Caterpillars start as eggs.

Moths lay tiny eggs.

Many moths attach their eggs to the bottom of leaves. This helps keep the eggs safe. Eggs are the first stage in a moth's life.

Moth eggs hatch into caterpillars.

A caterpillar is the second stage in a moth's life. Scientists call this stage "larva." Many other insect eggs hatch into larva, too.

Eating helps caterpillars.

Caterpillars eat a lot!

Caterpillars need lots of energy to grow for the third stage of their life cycle. To get this energy, they eat almost all the time.

Caterpillars eat leaves.

A caterpillar's favorite food is leaves. But if there are too many caterpillars eating a plant's leaves, the plant can die.

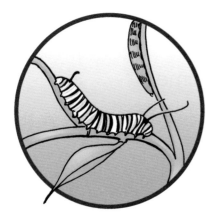

Color helps caterpillars.

Color can hide caterpillars.

Many caterpillars are the color of the plants they eat. They blend in so they are hard to see. This helps keep them safe.

Color can warn predators.

Other caterpillars are easy to see. Their colors warn birds and other predators that they taste bad. This helps keep them safe.

WHAT I LEARNED - part 1

Discuss the story with your team, then answer the questions below.

1 What is the first stage of a moth's life? What is the second?

_____

_____

_____

_____

_____

2 What do caterpillars do most of the time? Why?

_____

_____

_____

_____

_____

3 What are two different ways color can help caterpillars?

_____

_____

_____

_____

_____

DO THE ACTIVITY

Working with your research team, carefully follow each step below. Before you start, be sure you know the **safety rules** for this activity.

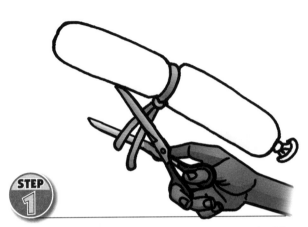

STEP 1

Inflate the balloon and **tie** the end. **Wrap** a piece of yarn around its center. **Pull** gently on the ends of the yarn until it begins to dent the balloon slightly. **Tie** the yarn and **cut** the ends.

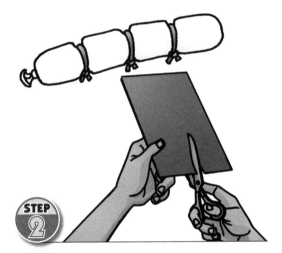

STEP 2

Use more yarn (**repeat** Step 1) to **divide** each of the balloon's two halves in half. Now **cut** a strip of construction paper four inches wide and the same length as your balloon.

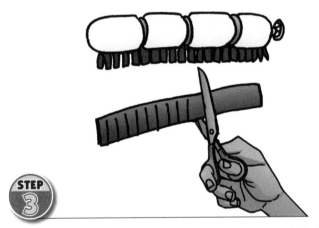

STEP 3

Fold the paper down the middle lengthwise. Now **cut** slits about a quarter inch apart up to the fold line. (Don't cut through the fold!) **Open** the paper and **attach** it to the balloon to make legs.

STEP 4

Decorate your balloon to look like caterpillars you have seen (in nature, books, or on TV). **Compare** your caterpillar with the ones that were created by other research teams.

WHAT I LEARNED - part 2

Discuss the activity with your team, then answer the questions below.

1 How is your caterpillar the same as other teams' caterpillars?

_____

_____

_____

_____

2 How is your caterpillar different from real caterpillars?

_____

_____

_____

_____

3 How could you change your caterpillar to look like a moth?

_____

_____

_____

_____

SHOW WHAT YOU KNOW - 1

Color the moth's **eggs** light green or white. Color the **caterpillar** dark green. Color the adult **moth** brown. Write these names on the correct line below.

This is a

_____

- - - - - - - - - - - - -

_____

These are

_____

- - - - - - - - - - - - -

_____

This is a

_____

- - - - - - - - - - - - -

_____

To the Parent . . .   **Scripture Connection:** Genesis 1:24-25

Lesson Focus:
Life Cycles

Lesson Objective:
To explore the larva stage of a moth's life cycle

National Science Education Standards:
Standard C2 — *"All students should develop an understanding of the life cycles of organisms . . . Organisms have life cycles that include being born, developing into adults, reproducing, and eventually dying . . ."*

Follow-up Questions:
Ask your child to describe a caterpillar. Ask how caterpillars are related to moths (caterpillars can turn into moths).
Ask your child what a caterpillar does most of the time. Ask why the caterpillar does this (eats; to get energy for "stage 3").
Ask your child how color can help a caterpillar (can help it hide from predators; can warn predators it tastes bad).

FOCUS Life Cycles (pupa)

OBJECTIVE To explore the pupa stage of a moth's life cycle

OVERVIEW When caterpillars have stored enough energy, they enter the third stage of the moth life cycle. In the "pupa" stage, they create and live in a special place called a "cocoon."

WHAT TO DO

With your team, carefully follow each step below.

Observe

Look closely at the cocoon your teacher is holding.

Look at its color. **Look** at its shape. How is it different from a caterpillar? How is it different from a moth?

Describe

Describe the cocoon. What does it **look** like?

What color is the cocoon? What shape is it?

What do you think the cocoon might **feel** like?

Discuss

What might be inside the cocoon? caterpillar

How does its color help the caterpillar? hides

What do you think is happening inside? changes

READ THE STORY

A **cocoon** is only one part of the life cycle of a **moth**. Read the story below to find out more about this stage in the moth's life.

Cocoons

A cocoon starts one stage in a moth's life.

Insects often change into different forms as they grow. Scientists call this a life cycle. Moths go through four stages: egg, larva, pupa, adult. Then the cycle repeats itself.

Caterpillars make cocoons.

Caterpillars start as eggs.

To begin the life cycle, moths lay tiny eggs (stage 1). These eggs hatch into larva called caterpillars (stage 2).

Caterpillars make cocoons.

To start the pupa stage (stage 3), the caterpillar makes itself a cocoon. A cocoon is a kind of sleeping bag for caterpillars.

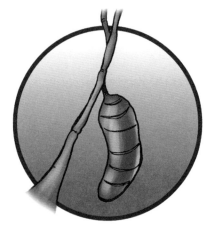

Cocoons help caterpillars.

Cocoons help caterpillars hide.

Cocoons blend in with their surroundings. This helps keep the caterpillar from being eaten while it hides inside.

Cocoons help caterpillars rest.

In the cocoon, the caterpillar does not eat. It moves very little and lives on energy it has stored up (during stage 2).

Cocoons change caterpillars.

Cocoons help caterpillars change.

The caterpillar is called a pupa now. The cocoon gives the pupa a safe place to live while it makes big changes.

Caterpillars change a lot!

Imagine getting into a sleeping bag, then coming out weeks later as an adult! A caterpillar's change is a lot like that.

WHAT I LEARNED - part 1

Discuss the story with your team, then answer the questions below.

1 What is the third stage of a moth's life? How is it covered?

_____

_____

_____

_____

_____

2 What does the pupa do while inside the cocoon?

_____

_____

_____

_____

_____

3 What might happen if a cocoon was not well hidden?

_____

_____

_____

_____

_____

DO THE ACTIVITY

Working with your research team, carefully follow each step below. Before you start, be sure you know the **safety rules** for this activity.

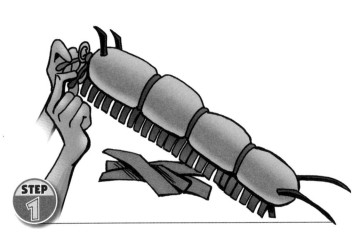

STEP 1

Cut tissue paper into strips about 1 inch wide. Now **tie** a piece of yarn to the end of your balloon caterpillar (created in Lesson 4). Make sure the yarn is secure.

STEP 2

Mix flour and water together to make a thin paste. **Dip** a strip of tissue paper in the paste. Carefully **lay** the wet paper on your caterpillar and **smooth** it down.

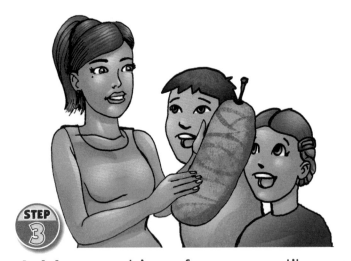

STEP 3

Add more strips of paper until your caterpillar is completely covered. (Keep the yarn free.) **Ask** your teacher to help you hang your new cocoon to dry.

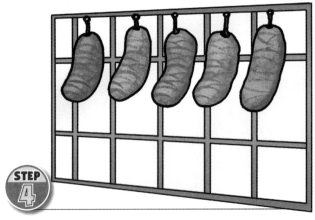

STEP 4

Compare your cocoon with the ones that were created by the other research teams. **Discuss** how it is like a real cocoon, and how it is not.

WHAT I LEARNED - part 2

Discuss the activity with your team, then answer the questions below.

1 How is your cocoon the same as other teams' cocoons?

_____

_____

_____

_____

_____

_____

2 How is your cocoon different from a real cocoon?

_____

_____

_____

_____

_____

_____

3 What might happen to your caterpillar if your cocoon were real?

_____

_____

_____

_____

_____

_____

NAME _____

SHOW WHAT YOU KNOW - 1

Color the **plant** a pretty green. Color the **cocoon** the same color green. Draw an arrow to where the **pupa** is hiding. Write these names on the correct line below.

The cocoon is attached to the

_____

- - - - - - - - - - - - - - - - - - - -

_____

Here is the

_____

- - - - - - - - - - - - - - - - - - - -

_____

Hiding inside is a

_____

- - - - - - - - - - - - - - - - - - - -

_____

To the Parent . . .   **Scripture Connection:** Isaiah 32:2

Lesson Focus:
Life Cycles (pupa)

Lesson Objective:
To explore the pupa stage of a moth's life cycle

National Science Education Standards:
Standard C2 — *"All students should develop an understanding of the life cycles of organisms . . . Organisms have life cycles that include being born, developing into adults, reproducing, and eventually dying . . ."*

Follow-up Questions:
Ask your child to describe a cocoon. Ask why cocoons are important to moths (help them hide, help them rest).
Ask your child what a pupa does inside the cocoon (changes from a caterpillar into a moth).
Ask your child how color can keep a cocoon hidden. Ask how this keeps the pupa safe (predators can't find it).

FOCUS   Life Cycles (adult)

OBJECTIVE   To explore the adult stage of a moth's life cycle

OVERVIEW   When the pupa emerges from the cocoon, it begins stage 4 of the moth life cycle (adult). The adult looks very different from the larva that entered the cocoon. Now it can even fly!

WHAT TO DO

With your team, carefully follow each step below.

Observe

Look at pictures of moths, or **think** about a moth you have seen (in nature, books, or on TV). How are moths and caterpillars different?

Describe

Describe a moth. What does it **look** like?

What color is it? What shape is it? What do you think a moth might **feel** like if it crawled on your hand?

Discuss

What did a moth used to look like? caterpillar

Name something moths do that caterpillars can't. fly

Where does a pupa change into a moth? cocoon

An adult **moth** is only one part of a complete insect life cycle. Read the story below to find out more about this stage of a moth's life.

Moths

An adult moth is one stage in a complete insect life cycle.

Insects often change into different forms as they grow. Scientists call this a life cycle. Moths go through four stages: egg, larva, pupa, and adult. Then the cycle repeats.

This moth is changing.

Big changes happen in the cocoon.

Inside the cocoon, the larva completely changes its form and turns into an adult. Scientists call this process "metamorphosis."

Changes are part of the life cycle.

A moth makes many changes in its life — from a moth egg, to a caterpillar (larva), to a pupa (in a cocoon), to an adult moth.

These are adult moths.

There are many kinds of moths.

Some moths live in the forest. Some live in vegetable fields. Some even live around piles of old clothes!

Moths are different from butterflies.

Moths have stout, hairy bodies. Their antennae look feathery. They fly mostly at night. When they rest, their wings lie flat.

The life cycle goes on.

Moths eventually die.

The life of a moth is short compared to human life. Soon it will die. But before they die, some moths will lay eggs.

Moths' eggs continue the life cycle.

When moths lay eggs, the moth life cycle starts all over again. Soon there is a new generation growing and changing.

WHAT I LEARNED - part 1

Discuss the story with your team, then answer the questions below.

1 What are the four stages of a moth's life cycle?

_____

_____

_____

_____

_____

_____

2 How are moths like butterflies? How are they different?

_____

_____

_____

_____

_____

_____

3 What might happen if moths stopped laying eggs?

_____

_____

_____

_____

_____

_____

DO THE ACTIVITY

Working with your research team, carefully follow each step below. Before you start, be sure you know the **safety rules** for this activity.

STEP 1

Look at the different moths on page 42, or **think** about a moth you have seen. Working with your team, **color** the wings and body of your moth to look like one of these moths.

STEP 2

Carefully **cut** the wings out of the sheet of paper. **Color** any areas that still need it. Now **glue** the wings to the body of your moth. Make sure they are straight while they dry.

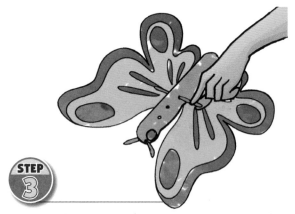

STEP 3

Cut three pipe cleaners in half. **Push** the pieces into the body to make six legs. **Wind** a pipe cleaner around a pencil. **Remove**, then **cut** in half. **Push** the curled pieces in (one for each antenna).

STEP 4

Compare your moth model with those created by other research teams. **Discuss** what the models have in common. How are the models like real moths? How are they different?

WHAT I LEARNED - part 2

Discuss the activity with your team, then answer the questions below.

1 How is your moth model like other team's models?

_____

_____

_____

_____

2 How is your moth model different from real moths?

_____

_____

_____

_____

3 What would you do differently to make a butterfly model?

_____

_____

_____

_____

SHOW WHAT YOU KNOW - 1

Color the moth **eggs** light green. Color the **caterpillar** dark green. Color the **cocoon** light brown. Color the **moth** dark brown. Write the names on the lines below.

This is a _____

_____

These are moth _____

_____

This is a _____

_____

This is a _____

_____

To the Parent . . .   **Scripture Connection:** Genesis 1:20-21

Lesson Focus:
Life Cycles (adult)

Lesson Objective:
To explore the adult stage of a moth's life cycle

National Science Education Standards:
Standard C2 — *"All students should develop an understanding of the life cycles of organisms . . . Organisms have life cycles that include being born, developing into adults, reproducing, and eventually dying . . ."*

Follow-up Questions:
Ask your child to name and describe the four stages of a moth's life cycle — egg, larva (caterpillar), pupa (cocoon), adult.
Ask your child how a moth is different from a butterfly (moths = stout bodies, feathery antenna, fly at night, etc.).
Show your child a real moth (in nature or on video). Ask them to tell you about moths (answers will vary).

FOCUS Camouflage

OBJECTIVE To explore how blending in with the environment protects a creature

OVERVIEW Many creatures need protection from predators that might eat them. If they blend in with their surroundings, they are much harder to see. This helps keep them hidden and safe.

WHAT TO DO

With your team, carefully follow each step below.

Observe

Look at the fish on page 48. **Look** at the bug on page 48. **Look** at the rabbit on page 48. **Think** about how each creature is like its surroundings.

Describe

Describe a fish you have seen (in nature, a book, or on TV). What did it **look** like? What **color** was it? What do you think a fish would **feel** like?

Discuss

What is one way a creature can blend in? color

What does blending in help a creature do? hide

What might a creature hide from? predator

Many creatures need protection from predators. Read the story below to find out how blending in with their surroundings helps keep creatures safe.

Hidden Creatures

Color helps many creatures hide.

Many creatures use color to help them hide from predators. They blend in with their surroundings so they are hard to see. Scientists call this coloring "camouflage."

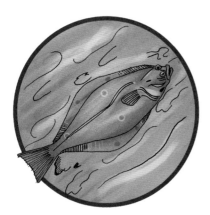

A fish can hide.

A fish can be tan like the sand.

The halibut is a fish that lives in the ocean where it is very sandy. A halibut is speckled tan. This helps it blend in with the sand.

Many fish use color to hide.

A scorpion fish looks like a rock. A flounder can change from dark colors to light. Some fish even match seaweed colors.

A bug can hide.

A bug can be green like a leaf.

Green leaf bugs live on green plants. Since they are the same color as the plant, they are very hard to see.

Leaf bugs are different colors.

Red leaf bugs live on red plants. Brown leaf bugs live on brown plants. Every leaf bug is the same color as the plant it lives on.

A rabbit can hide.

A rabbit can be brown like old grass.

Most rabbits live where there is lots of grass. Their fur is brown with dots and streaks so they blend in with old, brown grass.

Some rabbits can change color.

Some rabbits live where there is lots of snow. In the winter, their fur turns white. This helps them blend in with the snow.

WHAT I LEARNED - part 1

Discuss the story with your team, then answer the questions below.

1 How can creatures use color to help them hide?

_____

_____

_____

_____

_____

2 How are all leaf bugs similar? How are they different?

_____

_____

_____

_____

_____

_____

3 What might happen if a halibut swam over solid black rocks?

_____

_____

_____

_____

_____

DO THE ACTIVITY

Working with your research team, carefully follow each step below. Before you start, be sure you know the **safety rules** for this activity.

STEP 1

Cut out four red fish and four blue fish. **Place** one of these fish on a piece of newspaper. **Trace** around it to make an outline, then **cut out** the fish. **Repeat** to make three more "news" fish.

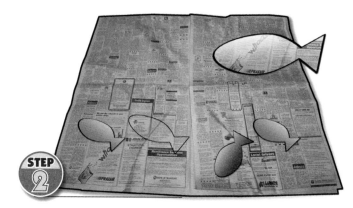

STEP 2

Lay a large sheet of newspaper on the floor. Ask your team to turn around. **Scatter** several fish on the newspaper. Now have everyone **glance** at the newspaper, then look away.

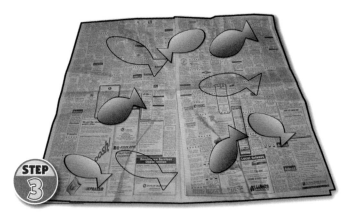

STEP 3

When everyone has had a turn, have them **guess** how many fish were there. If time permits, **repeat** step 2 using a different number of fish each time.

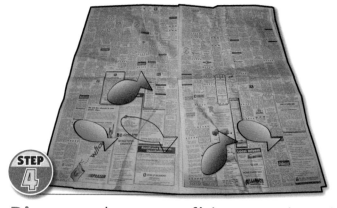

STEP 4

Discuss why some fish were hard to see. Why might its surroundings be important to a creature? **Compare** your observations with other teams.

WHAT I LEARNED - part 2

Discuss the activity with your team, then answer the questions below.

1 Why might a creature's surroundings be important?

_____

_____

_____

_____

2 How were the fish the same? How were they different?

_____

_____

_____

_____

3 How would this activity change if the floor sheet were red?

_____

_____

_____

_____

SHOW WHAT YOU KNOW - 1

Color the **fish** and the sand tan. Color the **leaf bug** and plant green. Color the **rabbit** and grass brown. Write the correct names on the line below.

Hiding on the leaf is a
_____
_____

Hiding in the grass is a
_____
_____

Hiding in the sand is a
_____
_____

To the Parent . . .   **Scripture Connection:** Psalms 17:8

Lesson Focus:
Camouflage

Lesson Objective:
To explore how blending with the environment helps protect a creature

National Science Education Standards:
Standard C3 — *"All students should develop an understanding of organisms and environments . . . patterns of behavior are related to the nature of the organism's environment . . . all organisms cause changes in the environment where they live . . ."*

Follow-up Questions:
Ask your child how color can help creatures hide (it helps them blend into their surroundings).
Ask your child why hiding is important to some creatures. What are they hiding from? (keeps them safe; predators).
Ask your child to name a creature they have studied, then describe how it hides (examples were fish, bugs, and rabbits).

FOCUS   Habitats

OBJECTIVE   To understand how creatures interact with their environment

OVERVIEW   Every creature has a special type of home (habitat). A creature's habitat must meet its unique needs. Different types of birds build different nests to help create their special habitats.

WHAT TO DO

With your team, carefully follow each step below.

Observe

Look at your home. **Think** about how it was made.

Now **look** at the birds' nests on page 54. **Think** about how each of these nests was made.

Describe

Describe a bird's nest that you have seen. What did it **look** like? What **color** was it? What was it made from? What do you think it would **feel** like?

Discuss

What word means an animal's home?   habitat

What kind of home do most birds build?   nest

What might be in a bird nest in the spring?   eggs

A **nest** is an important part of a bird's habitat. Read the story below to find out how different birds build different nests to meet their special needs.

Bird Nests

Different kinds of birds build different nests.

Different kinds of birds have different needs. Every kind of bird builds a different kind of nest that is specifically designed to meet that bird's needs.

This nest is in a tree.

Many birds build nests in trees.

A large area filled with trees is called a forest. Many kinds of birds live in the forest. Most forest birds build nests in trees.

Birds need the trees.

A nest built high in a tree helps keep birds safe from many kinds of predators. The leafy branches also help hide the nest.

This nest is in the prairie.

Many birds build nests in the prairie.

A prairie is a huge area with few trees. Many kinds of birds live in the prairie. Most prairie birds build nests in tall grass.

Birds need the prairie.

The prairie provides lots of food for birds. The tall grass helps hide the birds. It also gives them material to build their nests.

This nest is in a marsh.

Many birds build nests in a marsh.

A marsh is a large area covered with shallow water. Many kinds of birds live in the marsh. Most build nests in the reeds.

Birds need the marsh.

The marsh gives birds food and shelter. Sometimes a marsh is set aside just for birds. This is called a conservation area.

WHAT I LEARNED - part 1

Discuss the story with your team, then answer the questions below.

1 Why do birds build different kinds of nests?

_____

_____

_____

_____

_____

_____

2 How are forest nests like prairie nests? How are they different?

_____

_____

_____

_____

_____

_____

3 What might happen to marsh birds if the marsh dried up?

_____

_____

_____

_____

_____

_____

DO THE ACTIVITY

Working with your research team, carefully follow each step below. Before you start, be sure you know the **safety rules** for this activity.

STEP 1

Place a piece of wax paper on your work table. Carefully **stack** toothpicks on it in a small circle to make a nest. When finished, gently **move** this nest aside.

STEP 2

Repeat step 1, only this time try to **weave** yarn and feathers into the nest to help hold the toothpicks together. When finished, gently **move** this nest aside.

STEP 3

In a bowl, **mix** flour and water to make a thick "mud." **Dump** the mud on the paper, then **mold** it into the shape of a nest. **Add** a lining of feathers.

STEP 4

Observe your three nests. **Place** the eggs in each nest to see how they look. **Compare** the nests you made with those created by other research teams.

WHAT I LEARNED - part 2

Discuss the activity with your team, then answer the questions below.

1 Describe three different kinds of nests.

_____

_____

_____

_____

_____

_____

2 How were your nests the same? How were they different?

_____

_____

_____

_____

_____

_____

3 If a nest is destroyed, what might happen to the eggs? Why?

_____

_____

_____

_____

_____

_____

SHOW WHAT YOU KNOW - 1

Color the **forest** nest gray. Color the **prairie** nest brown. Color the **marsh** nest green. Write the names of each habitat on the correct line below.

This nest is in the

_____

This nest is in the

_____

This nest is in the

_____

To the Parent . . .   Scripture Connection: Psalms 84:3

Lesson Focus:
Habitats

Lesson Objective:
To understand how creatures interact with their environment

National Science Education Standards:
Standard C3 — *"All students should develop an understanding of organisms and environments . . . patterns of behavior are related to the nature of the organism's environment . . . all organisms cause changes in the environment where they live . . ."*

Follow-up Questions:
Ask your child to describe one type of bird's nest (see lesson ... answers will vary).
Ask your child why different kinds of birds make different kinds of nests (to meet their different needs).
Ask your child why nests are an important part of a bird's habitat (hide eggs, keep eggs safe, give birds shelter, etc.).

FOCUS Pollutants

OBJECTIVE To explore how pollutants impact the environment and living creatures

OVERVIEW Oil is an important resource. It provides fuel for cars, heat for homes, and many other good things. But oil in the wrong place is very harmful to living creatures. In this activity we'll explore what happens to birds in an oil spill.

WHAT TO DO

With your team, carefully follow each step below.

Observe

Look at the oil. **Look** at the water. **Look** at the feather.

Think about how oil and water are alike. **Think** about how oil and water are different.

Describe

Describe the oil. What does it **look** like? What does it **smell** like? What does it **feel** like? How is the feel of oil **different** from the feel of water?

Discuss

Which item works best for taking a bath? water

Which item would be helpful in cooking? oil

Which item is from a living creature? feather

READ THE STORY

Oil is an important resource. But oil in the wrong place can be very harmful to many living creatures. Read the story below to find out how.

Oil Spill

An oil spill can be very harmful.

When a big ship (tanker) that carries oil has an accident, oil can get into the ocean. This is called an "oil spill." Loose oil in the ocean can be very harmful.

Oil can hurt birds.

Oil can cover a bird's feathers.

In an oil spill, seabirds get oil on their feathers as they swim. The oil makes their feathers heavy so they cannot fly.

Oil can make a bird very sick.

When a seabird tries to clean oil off its feathers, it may eat some of the oil. The bird can become sick or even die.

Oil can hurt animals.

Oil can cover an animal's fur.

When there is an oil spill, animals that swim in the ocean can get oil on their fur. Oily fur cannot keep the animal warm.

Oil can make an animal very sick.

Oil can also get in the animal's lungs or stomach. This poisons the animal. It can become sick or even die.

Oil can hurt plants.

Oil can cover a plant's surface.

When there is an oil spill, oil can wash up on the shore. It can cover the shoreline grasses. It also can damage seaweed.

The fewer oil spills, the better!

The effects of an oil spill last a long time. New laws and new kinds of ships may lead to fewer oil spills in the future.

WHAT I LEARNED - part 1

Discuss the story with your team, then answer the questions below.

1 Why is an oil spill harmful to the environment?

_____

_____

_____

_____

2 How does an oil spill affect birds and animals differently?

_____

_____

_____

_____

3 What might happen to a pelican after an oil spill? Why?

_____

_____

_____

_____

DO THE ACTIVITY

Working with your research team, carefully follow each step below. Before you start, be sure you know the **safety rules** for this activity.

STEP 1

Label two cups "A" and "B." **Fill** both cups with water. (The cups represent two tiny oceans.) Now carefully **pour** three spoons of oil into Cup B. (This represents an oil spill.) **Compare** the cups.

STEP 2

Dip one feather in Cup A. (This represents a bird swimming in clean water.) **Remove** the feather and **blow** on it softly. **Make notes** about what you see.

STEP 3

Dip the other feather in Cup B. (This represents a bird swimming in an oil spill.) **Remove** the feather and **blow** on it softly. **Make notes** about what you see.

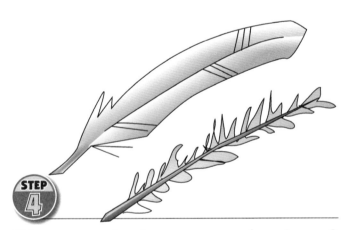

STEP 4

Discuss what you saw in step 2 and step 3 with your research team. Now **compare** your findings with those of other teams. How were the results similar?

WHAT I LEARNED - part 2

Discuss the activity with your team, then answer the questions below.

1 Describe what happened to the feather in step 3.

_____

_____

_____

_____

2 How were Cup A and Cup B similar? How were they different?

_____

_____

_____

_____

3 Would the Cup B feather improve over time? Why or why not?

_____

_____

_____

_____

SHOW WHAT YOU KNOW - 1

Color the **water** blue. Color the **oil spill** black. Color the **birds** white. Color the **animals** brown. Write the correct names on the lines below.

This is an

_____

_ _ _ _ _ _ _ _ _ _ _ _ _ _ _

An oil spill can hurt

_____

_ _ _ _ _ _ _ _ _ _ _ _ _ _ _

An oil spill can hurt

_____

_ _ _ _ _ _ _ _ _ _ _ _ _ _ _

To the Parent . . .   **Scripture Connection:** 1 Corinthians 15:33

Lesson Focus:
Pollutants

Lesson Objective:
To explore how pollutants impact the environment and living creatures

National Science Education Standards:
Standard C3 — *"All students should develop an understanding of organisms and environments . . . patterns of behavior are related to the nature of the organism's environment . . . all organisms cause changes in the environment where they live . . ."*

Follow-up Questions:
Ask your child what might cause an oil spill in the ocean (a big ship that carries oil might have an accident).
Ask your child how an oil spill can hurt seabirds (can't fly; when they try to clean feathers, it makes them sick; etc.).
Ask your child how an oil spill can hurt sea animals (oily fur can't keep animal warm; oil can poison the animal, etc.).

Earth

LESSONS 10-18

Earth

Earth Science

Earth Science is the study of **earth** and **sky**. In this section, you'll explore the structure of our planet (rocks, fossils, etc.), and patterns of change on Earth (days, nights, months, years). We'll even take a look at the solar system, and what causes an eclipse.

FOCUS   Earth Materials

OBJECTIVE   To explore differences between natural and manufactured materials

OVERVIEW   Some materials like sand or soil occur naturally on Earth. Others like plastic, paper, or glass are manufactured. The manufacturing process changes natural materials in some way.

WHAT TO DO

With your team, carefully follow each step below.

Observe

Look at each material carefully. **Think** about where it came from. How are these materials similar to each other? How are they different?

Describe

Describe each material. What does it **look** like? What does it **feel** like? What **color** is it? What **shape** is it? What might it be used for?

Discuss

What is one common natural material? sand

What is one manufactured material? plastic

Name another manufactured material. paper

There are many kinds of materials on Earth. Some are natural; some are manufactured. Read the story below to learn how they are different.

Earth Materials

There are many kinds of materials on Earth.

Some materials (sand, soil, etc.) occur naturally on Earth. Other materials (glass, paper, plastic, etc.) are manufactured by changing natural materials in some way.

These are natural materials.

There are many natural materials.

A natural material is one that has not been changed by man. These resources are sometimes called "raw materials."

Sand is a natural material.

Sand is an example of a natural material. It is commonly found on the banks of some rivers or along the ocean shore.

These are manufactured materials.

There are many manufactured materials.

A product is "manufactured" when natural materials and other ingredients are processed to make something different.

Paper is a manufactured material.

Paper is an example of a manufactured material. Although wood occurs naturally, it must be processed to make paper.

Earth materials are resources.

Some resources are renewable.

Some materials can be used over and over (recycled). For example, a managed forest is a renewable source of wood.

Some resources are not renewable.

When some natural materials are gone, they will be gone forever. Oil is an example of a non-renewable resource.

WHAT I LEARNED - part 1

Discuss the story with your team, then answer the questions below.

1 Name two kinds of materials. Give an example of each.

_____

_____

_____

_____

_____

_____

2 How are natural and manufactured materials different?

_____

_____

_____

_____

_____

_____

3 How might your life change if there were no more oil or gas?

_____

_____

_____

_____

DO THE ACTIVITY

Working with your research team, carefully follow each step below. Before you start, be sure you know the **safety rules** for this activity.

STEP 1

Place all the materials on your work surface. **Examine** each material closely. **Discuss** which might be natural and which might be manufactured.

STEP 2

Now **separate** the materials into two groups — one for natural materials; one for manufactured materials. **Make** a list of the items in each group.

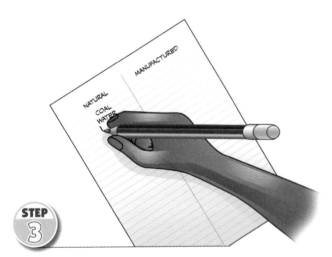

STEP 3

Make a second list of natural and manufactured materials that are not in your kit. **Discuss** other items that might be difficult to classify this way.

STEP 4

Review each step in this activity. **Discuss** how the materials were alike and different. Now **compare** your lists with those of the other research teams.

WHAT I LEARNED - part 2

Discuss the activity with your team, then answer the questions below.

1 Give three examples of natural and manufactured materials.

_____

_____

_____

_____

_____

2 How are the twig and craft stick similar? How are they different?

_____

_____

_____

_____

_____

3 How would life be different without manufactured materials?

_____

_____

_____

_____

_____

SHOW WHAT YOU KNOW - 1

Circle manufactured materials in red. Circle natural materials in blue. (Remember, materials we can use are resources.) Write the correct names on the line below.

Some materials are

_____

_____

craft stick

notebook paper

balloon

Some materials are

_____

_____

pea gravel

Materials we use are

_____

_____

twig

sand

To the Parent . . .　　　　　　　　　　**Scripture Connection:** Psalms 8:3-4

Lesson Focus:
Earth Materials

Lesson Objective:
To explore differences between natural and manufactured materials

National Science Education Standards:
Standard D1 — *"All students should develop an understanding of the properties of earth materials . . . their different physical and chemical properties . . . which make them useful in various ways . . ."*

Follow-up Questions:
Ask your child to give two examples of a natural material (anything not processed by man).
Ask your child to give two examples of a manufactured material (anything made in a factory or otherwise processed).
Ask your child why it's important to conserve non-renewable natural resources (when they are gone, they are gone).

FOCUS   Geology

OBJECTIVE   To understand that different rocks have different characteristics

OVERVIEW   There are many kinds of "rocks," but not all rocks are alike. Rocks can be smooth or rough, dull or full of beautiful colors. In this activity, we'll look at three very different and unusual rocks.

WHAT TO DO

With your team, carefully follow each step below.

- -

Observe

Look at Rock 1 (pyrite). Look at Rock 2 (wonderstone).

Look at Rock 3 (pumice). Think about how these rocks

are the same. Think about how they are different.

- -

Describe

Describe each rock. What does it look like?

What color is it? What does it feel like? What shape is it?

Is it heavier or lighter than the other rocks?

- -

Discuss

Which rock has layers of color? wonderstone

Which rock is the lightest rock? pumice

Which rock looks a lot like gold? pyrite

There are many kinds of rocks on Earth, but rocks can be very different. Read the story below to learn about three very different rocks.

Wonderful Rocks

Rocks can be very different.

There are many kinds of rocks. They can be hard or soft, light or heavy, smooth or rough. They come in many colors. Different rocks can be used in different ways.

This is pyrite.

Pyrite is a common mineral.

Iron pyrite is very hard. Because of its rich golden color, iron pyrite is sometimes called "fool's gold."

Pyrite has many uses.

Pyrite is an important source of the chemical sulphur. It is also prized by rock collectors, and is even used in jewelry.

This is pumice.

Pumice comes from volcanoes.

Some lava is filled with gases. When it spews from a volcano, it creates rocks full of holes from trapped gas bubbles.

Pumice has many uses.

Pumice is an ingredient in concrete blocks. It's also used for agriculture, cleaning abrasives, and even aging blue jeans.

This is wonderstone.

Wonderstone comes from sand.

Wonderstone is a type of sandstone that has beautiful colors. Sandstone is sand turned to rock. It is formed in many layers.

Wonderstone can be decorative.

Since it is relatively soft, wonderstone is often shaped and carved to make bookends, drink coasters, and more.

Discuss the story with your team, then answer the questions below.

1 Name at least one use for each rock in the story.

_____

_____

_____

_____

_____

2 How are pumice and pyrite similar? How are they different?

_____

_____

_____

_____

_____

_____

3 What might happen if you dropped a slab of sandstone? Why?

_____

_____

_____

_____

_____

DO THE ACTIVITY

Working with your research team, carefully follow each step below. Before you start, be sure you know the **safety rules** for this activity.

STEP 1

Look closely at the pyrite. **Make notes** about what you see (its color, shape, size, etc.). **Repeat** this process with the pumice, then the wonderstone.

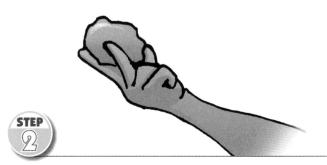

STEP 2

Rub the pyrite between your fingers and thumb. **Make notes** about what you feel (texture). **Repeat** this process with the pumice, then the wonderstone.

STEP 3

Fill a bowl with water. **Place** the pyrite in the water. **Record** the results. **Remove** and **dry** the pyrite, then **repeat** this step with the pumice, then the wonderstone.

STEP 4

Review each step in this activity. **Discuss** your observations with team members. Now **compare** your findings with those of other research teams.

WHAT I LEARNED - part 2

Discuss the activity with your team, then answer the questions below.

1 Name some ways that rocks can be different.

2 How are wonderstone and pyrite similar? How are they different?

3 Would a huge chunk of pumice still float? Why or why not?

SHOW WHAT YOU KNOW - 1

Color the pyrite gold. Color the pumice light grey.
Color the wonderstone with reds or browns. Write the correct names on the lines below.

This light, porous rock is

_____

_____

This colorful, layered rock is

_____

_____

This hard, golden rock is

_____

_____

To the Parent . . .   **Scripture Connection:** Matthew 7:24-27

Lesson Focus:
Geology

Lesson Objective:
To understand that different rocks have different characteristics

National Science Education Standards:
Standard D1 — *"All students should develop an understanding of the properties of Earth materials . . . their different physical and chemical properties . . . which make them useful in various ways . . ."*

Follow-up Questions:
Ask your child to describe pyrite. Ask what other name it is sometimes called (fool's gold).
Ask your child to describe pumice. Ask what is unusual about this rock (it floats).
Ask your child to describe wonderstone. Ask what it is often used for (to make decorative items).

FOCUS Fossils

OBJECTIVE To explore how mold fossils were created

OVERVIEW Fossils are remains (bones, shells, etc.) of ancient living things. But fossils can also be imprints or "molds" (like a footprint or shape) that were left behind and preserved in the earth's crust.

WHAT TO DO

With your team, carefully follow each step below.

Observe

Look at the fossils on page 80. **Think** about other fossils that you have seen (in nature, books, or on TV). How are these fossils similar? How are they different?

Describe

Describe each fossil. What does it **look** like? What **color** is it? What might it **feel** like? What **shape** is it? How is it different from an ordinary rock?

Discuss

What are some ancient remains called? fossils

What is another name for a fossil imprint? mold

Name one thing an imprint might show. shape

There are many kinds of fossils on Earth. Fossils can be very different. Read the story below to learn about some different kinds of fossils.

Fossils

There are many kinds of fossils.

Fossils can be the petrified remains of ancient creatures or plants. But many fossils are an imprint (mold) of a creature's shape or a similar trace of their existence.

This is an animal fossil.

A fossil can be an animal part.

Since the soft parts of animals decompose quickly, animal fossils are usually just hard parts like shells, bones, or teeth.

An animal fossil can be stone.

Often an animal part is slowly replaced by minerals in the water around it. This makes an exact replica of the part in stone!

This is a plant fossil.

A fossil can be a plant part.

Some ancient plants were buried in sediment which became stone. Plant fossils include branches, seeds, and leaves.

A plant fossil can be stone.

Just like animal parts, plant parts can also be replaced by surrounding minerals, making an exact replica in stone.

This is a mold fossil.

Mold fossils are very common.

Many fossils are not actual animal or plant parts. They are imprints (molds), often made in ancient mud or sand.

One type of rock has many fossils.

Most fossils are found in "sedimentary" rock (mud or sand turned to stone). Limestone and sandstone are examples.

WHAT I LEARNED - part 1

Discuss the story with your team, then answer the questions below.

1 Name three kinds of fossils. Which fossil is the most common?

_____

_____

_____

_____

2 How are the fossils on page 80 similar? How are they different?

_____

_____

_____

_____

_____

3 What kind of fossil is easiest to find in sedimentary rock? Why?

_____

_____

_____

_____

DO THE ACTIVITY

Working with your research team, carefully follow each step below. Before you start, be sure you know the **safety rules** for this activity.

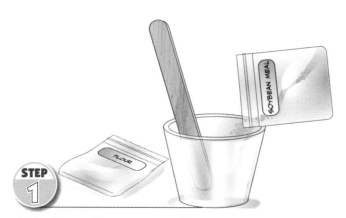

Stir the flour, soybean meal, and salt together in a bowl. Slowly **add** water to make a thick paste. (This represents sediment for your sedimentary rock.)

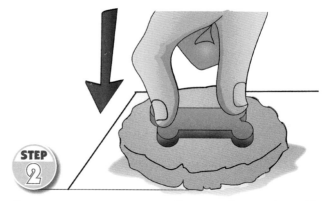

Scoop your sediment onto the wax paper and **flatten**. **Dip** the dog biscuit in flour. Now **press** it into the sediment to make an imprint (mold), then **remove**.

Set your "mold fossil" aside to dry overnight. If you wish, **repeat** step 1 and 2 of this activity using a toy creature (turtle, lizard, etc.) to see what kind of imprint it makes.

Review each step in this activity. **Discuss** your observations with team members. Now **compare** your "fossils" with those of other research teams.

WHAT I LEARNED - part 2

Discuss the activity with your team, then answer the questions below.

1 The "fossil" you created represents what kind of fossil?

_____

_____

_____

_____

2 How are mold fossils different from other kinds of fossils?

_____

_____

_____

_____

_____

3 Would an ancient footprint be a mold fossil? Why or why not?

_____

_____

_____

_____

_____

SHOW WHAT YOU KNOW - 1

Color the **animal** fossil in browns. Color the **plant** fossil in grays. Color the **mold** fossil in light reds. Write the correct names on the line below.

This fossil is called a
_____

This fossil is from a
_____

This fossil is from an
_____

To the Parent . . . **Scripture Connection:** Isaiah 64:8

Lesson Focus:
Fossils

Lesson Objective:
To explore how mold fossils were created

National Science Education Standards:
Standard D1 — *"All students should develop an understanding of the properties of earth materials . . . their different physical and chemical properties . . . which make them useful in various ways . . ."*

Follow-up Questions:
Ask your child to name three kinds of fossils (animal fossils, plant fossils, mold fossils).
Ask your child which fossil is the most common kind of fossil (the mold fossil).
Ask your child how a mold fossil is different from other fossils (a mold fossil is an imprint, not the thing itself).

FOCUS Solar System

OBJECTIVE To explore the relationship between the Sun, planets, and moons

OVERVIEW Objects in our solar system (the Sun, moons, and planets) have locations and movements that can be seen and described.

WHAT TO DO

With your team, carefully follow each step below.

Observe

Look at each planet carefully. Think about how it is like other planets. Think about how it is different. Look at the solar system. Think about how planets move.

Describe

Describe each planet. What does it look like? What color is it? What shape is it? How big is it compared to the other planets?

Discuss

What is at the center of the solar system? Sun

What is the third planet from the Sun? Earth

What object circles around Earth? Moon

A sun and its planets is called a solar system. There are many objects in our solar system. Read the story below to learn more about these objects.

Solar System

A sun and the objects circling it is called a solar system.

Our solar system consists of a star we call "the Sun" and nine planets. It also includes the moons around the planets, as well as comets, asteroids, and meteorites.

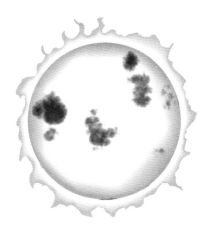

This is the Sun.

The Sun is the center of our solar system.

All the planets and other objects in our solar system orbit around the Sun. It takes Earth one full year to complete its orbit.

The Sun is very large and hot.

Over a million planets the size of Earth could fit inside the Sun. The Sun's surface has a temperature of over 11,000 degrees.

This is a planet.

Some planets are solid.

In our solar system, the four planets closest to the Sun are hard and rocky. They are Mercury, Mars, Earth, and Venus.

Some planets are mostly gas.

Except for Pluto, the other planets in our solar system are huge "gas giants." They are Jupiter, Saturn, Uranus, and Neptune.

This is a moon.

Moons circle some planets.

Moons are large natural objects that orbit planets. Some planets have many moons, but some have none at all.

Our moon is unusual.

Most moons are very tiny compared to the planets they circle. But Earth's moon is more than one-fourth as large as Earth!

Discuss the story with your team, then answer the questions below.

1 Name two kinds of planets. Give an example of each.

_____

_____

_____

_____

_____

_____

2 How is Earth's moon like other moons? How is it different?

_____

_____

_____

_____

_____

_____

3 What might happen if Earth moved closer to the Sun? Why?

_____

_____

_____

_____

_____

_____

DO THE ACTIVITY

Working with your research team, carefully follow each step below. Before you start, be sure you know the **safety rules** for this activity.

STEP 1

Using an encyclopedia or the Internet, **list** the nine planets in order. **Write** down how far each one is from the Sun. Now **discuss** which four planets are largest.

STEP 2

Your teacher will assign each team a planet, then give you a balloon. **Inflate** your balloon, then use construction paper to **make** a sign for your planet.

STEP 3

Follow your teacher to the football field. A punch ball on the goal line will represent the Sun. **Move** your "planet" to the spot your teacher indicates.

STEP 4

Predict how long it might take each team to walk in a circle around the Sun (staying at this distance). **Compare** your prediction with other teams'.

WHAT I LEARNED - part 2

Discuss the activity with your team, then answer the questions below.

1 Which two planets travel farthest to orbit the Sun? Why?

_____

_____

_____

_____

_____

_____

2 How are Pluto and Mercury similar? How are they different?

_____

_____

_____

_____

_____

_____

3 What might the temperature be like on Mercury? Why?

_____

_____

_____

_____

_____

SHOW WHAT YOU KNOW - 1

Circle the Sun with red. Circle the planet with blue. Circle the moon with brown. Write the correct names on the lines below.

At the center of the solar system is the

_____

_ _ _ _ _ _ _ _ _ _ _ _ _ _ _ _ _ _ _

Orbiting the Sun is a

_____

_ _ _ _ _ _ _ _ _ _ _ _ _ _ _ _ _ _ _

Orbiting the planet is a

_____

_ _ _ _ _ _ _ _ _ _ _ _ _ _ _ _ _ _ _

To the Parent . . .   Scripture Connection: Psalms 8:3-4

Lesson Focus:
Solar System

Lesson Objective:
To explore the relationship between the Sun, the planets, and moons.

National Science Education Standards:
Standard D2 — *"All students should develop an understanding of objects in the sky . . . the Sun, Moon, stars . . . all have properties, locations, and movements that can be observed and described . . ."*

Follow-up Questions:
Ask your child what object is at the center of the solar system (the Sun).
Ask your child about the relationship between the planets and the Sun (planets orbit the Sun).
Ask your child about the relationship between a moon and a planet (moons orbit planets).

FOCUS Eclipses

OBJECTIVE To explore how solar and lunar eclipses occur

OVERVIEW The movement of objects in our solar system can sometimes create unusual sights. Solar and lunar eclipses have fascinated people since the beginning of time.

WHAT TO DO

With your team, carefully follow each step below.

Observe

Think about pictures you have seen of the Sun, Moon, and Earth. **Think** about how they were alike. **Think** about how they were different.

Describe

Describe the Sun, Moon, and Earth. What does each one **look** like? What **color** is it? What **shape** is it? How **big** is it compared to the others?

Discuss

What do you think the Earth goes around? Sun

What do you think the Moon goes around? Earth

What can reflect the Sun's light at night? Moon

An **eclipse** happens when the Sun, Moon, and Earth line up in a certain way. Read the story below to learn more about eclipses.

Eclipse

An eclipse is like a giant shadow.

In our solar system, all light comes from the Sun. But sometimes the Earth or the Moon gets in the way. The light is blocked, making a huge shadow called an eclipse.

This is a solar eclipse.

The Moon blocks the Sun's light.

When the Moon's orbit moves it between the Earth and the Sun, it causes a solar eclipse. The Moon's shadow falls on the Earth.

A solar eclipse makes the day dark.

A solar eclipse only lasts a short time, but it makes the daytime sky turn dark. Birds and animals often think night has come!

This is a lunar eclipse.

The Earth blocks the Sun's light.

When the Earth's orbit moves it between the Moon and the Sun, it causes a lunar eclipse. The Earth's shadow falls on the Moon.

A lunar eclipse makes the Moon dark.

Since the Moon only reflects the light from the Sun, the Earth's shadow makes it turn dark. A dark moon looks very strange.

Scientists study eclipses.

Eclipses can be predicted.

Scientists know that the positions of the Sun, Moon, and Earth cause a solar or lunar eclipse about once every six months.

Lunar eclipses are easier to see.

Each solar eclipse only covers a tiny area of Earth. But a lunar eclipse can be seen from anywhere on Earth's night side.

Discuss the story with your team, then answer the questions below.

1 What causes a solar eclipse?

_____

_____

_____

_____

_____

_____

2 How are solar and lunar eclipses alike? How are they different?

_____

_____

_____

_____

_____

_____

3 What might a bird do during a solar eclipse? Why?

_____

_____

_____

_____

_____

DO THE ACTIVITY

Working with your research team, carefully follow each step below. Before you start, be sure you know the **safety rules** for this activity.

STEP 1

Push a dowel rod into both balls (large for Earth; small for Moon). **Ask** a team member to shine a flashlight directly at the "Earth" from about one foot away.

STEP 2

Slowly **move** the Moon behind the Earth. **Watch** as the Moon goes from light to dark as the shadow of the Earth covers it. (This models a lunar eclipse.)

STEP 3

Now **move** the Moon between the Earth and the Sun. **Watch** as the Moon's shadow moves across the Earth. (This models a solar eclipse.)

STEP 4

Discuss what an ant would have seen from your Earth during the simulated eclipses. **Compare** your observations with those of other research teams.

WHAT I LEARNED - part 2

Discuss the activity with your team, then answer the questions below.

1 What causes a lunar eclipse?

_____

_____

_____

_____

_____

_____

2 How were step 2 and step 3 similar? How were they different?

_____

_____

_____

_____

_____

_____

3 How can models like this help us understand how things work?

_____

_____

_____

_____

_____

SHOW WHAT YOU KNOW - 1

Circle the solar eclipse with red. Circle the lunar eclipse with blue. Write the correct names on the lines below.

This is a _____ eclipse.

This is a _____ eclipse.

To the Parent . . .   **Scripture Connection:** Psalms 91:4

Lesson Focus:
Eclipses

Lesson Objective:
To explore how solar and lunar eclipses occur

National Science Education Standards:
Standard D2 — *"All students should develop an understanding of objects in the sky . . . the Sun, Moon, stars . . . all have properties, locations, and movements that can be observed and described . . ."*

Follow-up Questions:
Ask your child what causes a solar eclipse (the Moon gets between Earth and the Sun).
Ask your child what causes a lunar eclipse (the Earth gets between the Sun and the Moon).
Ask your child which one is more commonly seen (lunar: they can be seen from anywhere on Earth's night side).

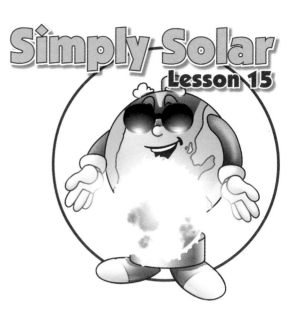

FOCUS Solar Energy

OBJECTIVE To explore how color can reflect or absorb sunlight

OVERVIEW Some colors reflect light. Some colors absorb light. When the light from the sun is absorbed, it can create heat energy.

WHAT TO DO

With your team, carefully follow each step below.

Observe

Look at the two tubes. Remove their caps and look inside. Think about how the tubes are similar. Think about how the tubes are different.

Describe

Describe the two tubes. What do they look like? What do they feel like? What shape are they? How strong are they? What color is each tube?

Discuss

What word can mean "bounce off"? reflect

What word can mean "to take in"? absorb

What can help reflect or absorb sunlight? color

Some colors **reflect** light. Some colors **absorb** light. Read the story below to find out what happens when sunlight strikes different colors.

Solar Energy

Scientists call energy from the Sun "solar energy."

Solar energy is created by sunlight. When sunlight is absorbed, it can create heat (one form of energy). An object's color can affect how much light it absorbs.

Light can create heat.

Heat *cannot* travel through space.

Even though the Sun is very hot, it is too far away for its heat to affect Earth. The heat of the Sun cannot reach us.

But light *can* travel through space.

Light from the Sun travels through space to strike the Earth. This light is absorbed by many objects on Earth.

Colors absorb or reflect light.

Dark colors can absorb sunlight.

Dark, dull colors (like flat black) can absorb light. When sunlight is absorbed, it can create heat, making an object hot.

Light colors can reflect sunlight.

Light, shiny colors (like glossy white) reflect light. When sunlight is reflected, it can keep an object from getting hot.

Colors can affect comfort.

A white shirt can help keep you cool.

Since white reflects sunlight, a white shirt keeps you cooler if you're in the sun. Many people wear white clothes in summer.

A black shirt can help keep you warm.

Since black absorbs sunlight, a black shirt can be warmer than a white shirt. Many people prefer dark clothes in the fall.

WHAT I LEARNED - part 1

Discuss the story with your team, then answer the questions below.

1 How can a dark color make something hot?

_____

_____

_____

_____

_____

2 How are black and white alike? How are they different?

_____

_____

_____

_____

_____

3 Which might keep you cooler on a hot day — a light yellow shirt or a dark blue one? Why?

_____

_____

_____

_____

DO THE ACTIVITY

Working with your research team, carefully follow each step below. Before you start, be sure you know the **safety rules** for this activity.

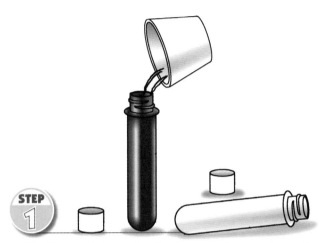

STEP 1

Fill the black tube almost full of water. (**Leave** about a half inch of air at the top.) **Replace** the cap and tighten it. **Repeat** with the white tube.

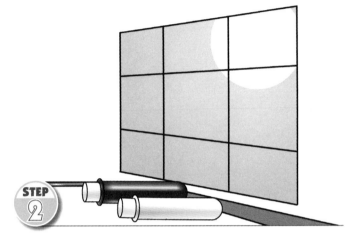

STEP 2

Place one sheet of white construction paper in the direct sun. **Lay** both tubes on the paper as shown. **Leave** the tubes in the sun for at least two hours.

STEP 3

Touch a finger to the water in the white tube to test its temperature. **Repeat** using the black tube. Make sure everyone on your team has a turn.

STEP 4

Discuss your findings. What was the only variable (difference) between the tubes? **Compare** your observations with those of other research teams.

WHAT I LEARNED - part 2

Discuss the activity with your team, then answer the questions below.

1 Where did the energy for this activity come from?

2 How were the two tubes alike? How were they different?

3 Which might be hotter inside — a black car or a white car? Why?

NAME _____

SHOW WHAT YOU KNOW - 1

Circle the objects that should **absorb** sunlight with red.
Circle the objects that should **reflect** sunlight with blue.
Write the correct names on the lines below.

Light objects _____ sunlight.

_ _ _ _ _ _ _ _ _ _ _ _ _ _ _ _

Dark objects _____ sunlight.

_ _ _ _ _ _ _ _ _ _ _ _ _ _ _ _

To the Parent . . .   **Scripture Connection:** Revelation 3:15

Lesson Focus:
Solar Energy

Lesson Objective:
To explore how color helps change sunlight into heat

National Science Education Standards:
Standard D2 — *"All students should develop an understanding of objects in the sky . . . the Sun, Moon, stars . . . the Sun provides the light and heat necessary to maintain the temperature of the Earth . . ."*

Follow-up Questions:
Ask your child how sunlight might affect a dull, black car (would absorb sunlight, might make it hotter, etc.).
Ask your child how sunlight might affect a shiny white car (would reflect sunlight, might make it cooler, etc.).
Ask your child why people prefer white or light-colored clothes in the summer (they reflect sunlight, making them cooler).

FOCUS Day and Night

OBJECTIVE To explore how Earth's rotation causes day and night

OVERVIEW As the Earth spins (rotates), different parts of the Earth face the Sun. This makes it seem as if the Sun is moving across the sky, creating what we call day and night.

WHAT TO DO

With your team, carefully follow each step below.

Observe

Look at the sky in the early morning. **Look** at the sky at noon. **Look** at the sky in the evening. **Think** about where the Sun appears at each of these times.

Describe

Describe the Sun in the morning, noon, and evening. What does it **look** like? How does it make the sky **change**? **Describe** different sunsets you have seen.

Discuss

What is the Earth's spin called? rotation

Where does the Sun appear in the morning? east

Where does the Sun appear at sunset? west

When a place on Earth faces the Sun, it is **day**. When it faces away from the Sun, it is **night**. Read the story below to learn more.

Day and Night

Earth circles the Sun.

Like the other planets in our solar system, the Earth circles the Sun. But as it circles the Sun, it also spins around and around. Scientists call this spinning motion "rotation."

Earth rotates.

One rotation takes 24 hours.

Even though it seems to be sitting still, the Earth is constantly rotating. It takes Earth 24 hours to spin around one time.

The Sun shines on Earth.

The Sun is always shining on the Earth. But as the Earth rotates, different parts face the Sun. This causes day and night.

This is day.

In the day, the sky is full of light.

When a place on Earth faces the Sun, the sky is full of light. We call this the day.

Day is an active time.

Most animals are active and awake during the day. Day is also when most humans work and play.

This is night.

At night, the sky is dark.

When a place on Earth does not face the Sun, the sky is dark. We call this the night.

Night is a quiet time.

Most animals are quiet and asleep during the night. Night is also when most humans rest and sleep.

WHAT I LEARNED - part 1

Discuss the story with your team, then answer the questions below.

1 What causes day and night?

_____

_____

_____

_____

_____

2 How is a cloudy day like night? How are they different?

_____

_____

_____

_____

_____

3 What might happen if the Earth rotated slower? Why?

_____

_____

_____

_____

_____

DO THE ACTIVITY

Working with your research team, carefully follow each step below. Before you start, be sure you know the **safety rules** for this activity.

STEP 1

Paint your ball to look like Earth. **Use** blue for water and green for land. **Paint** a little white at the top and bottom (for ice at the North and South poles).

STEP 2

Look at a globe. **Tilt** your Earth slightly like the globe, then **push** your Earth gently down onto the dowel rod. **Attach** a push pin to show where you live.

STEP 3

Stand about six feet from the lamp (dark room). Slowly **rotate** your Earth. **Look** where the light ends and **watch** the push pin move into and out of the light.

STEP 4

Discuss what an ant standing on the push pin would have seen from your Earth. **Compare** your observations with those of other research teams.

WHAT I LEARNED - part 2

Discuss the activity with your team, then answer the questions below.

1 What was moving in this activity? What was not moving?

_____

_____

_____

_____

_____

2 How is this model similar to Earth? How is it different?

_____

_____

_____

_____

_____

3 What might happen if the Earth stopped rotating? Why?

_____

_____

_____

_____

_____

SHOW WHAT YOU KNOW - 1

Circle in **red** the part of the Earth where it is **day**.
Circle in **blue** the part of the Earth where it is **night**.
Write the correct names on the lines below.

When a place on Earth
faces the Sun, it is

_____

_ _ _ _ _ _ _ _ _ _ _ _ _ _

_____

When a place on Earth
does not face the Sun, it is

_____

_ _ _ _ _ _ _ _ _ _ _ _ _ _

_____

To the Parent . . .   **Scripture Connection:** 2 Peter 3:8

Lesson Focus:
Day and Night

Lesson Objective:
To explore how Earth's rotation causes day and night

National Science Education Standards:
Standard D3 — *"All students should develop an understanding of changes in the Earth and sky . . . objects in the sky have patterns of movement . . . the Sun and Moon move across the sky on a daily basis . . ."*

Follow-up Questions:
Ask your child what it's called when a place on Earth faces the Sun (day).
Ask your child what it's called when a place on Earth does not face the Sun (night).
Ask your child what the Earth does that causes day and night (it spins around or "rotates").

FOCUS Moon Phases

OBJECTIVE To explore how a month relates to the Moon's movement around Earth

OVERVIEW A month is roughly equal to one complete trip (revolution) of the Moon around the Earth. Throughout the month, the Moon appears to change shapes.

WHAT TO DO

With your team, carefully follow each step below.

Observe

Look at the pictures of the Moon on page 110. **Think** about how these pictures are different. **Look** closely at the shape of the Moon in each picture.

Describe

Describe the Moon. What does it **look** like? What might its surface **feel** like? **Describe** different **shapes** or **colors** you've seen in the Moon on different nights.

Discuss

What large object circles around the Earth? Moon

About how long does one trip take? month

What seems to change about the Moon? shape

The time periods that we call **months** are roughly based on the movement of the **Moon** around the Earth. Read the story below to learn more.

Months and Moons

Ancient people used the Moon to measure time.

A month is a unit of time roughly based on how long it takes the Moon to circle Earth. In fact, the word "month" comes from an ancient word meaning "moon."

The Moon has phases.

The Moon seems to change shapes.

As it circles Earth, the Moon seems to change shapes. These different shapes are called "phases."

Each phase looks different.

This is because we see the bright part of the Moon from different angles. There are four major shapes in each cycle.

These are beginning phases.

This is the "new" Moon.

When the Moon is between the Sun and the Earth, we can not see the bright side of the Moon. The part facing us is dark.

This is the "first quarter" Moon.

A week after "new moon," the Moon is a quarter of the way around Earth. We can see only half of the bright part.

These are ending phases.

This is the "full" Moon.

Two weeks after "new moon," the Moon is halfway around Earth. Only now can we see all the bright side of the Moon.

This is the "last quarter" Moon.

Three weeks after "new moon," the Moon is three-quarters of the way around Earth. Soon the cycle will begin over again.

WHAT I LEARNED - part 1

Discuss the story with your team, then answer the questions below.

1 What is the relationship between the Moon and a month?

_____

_____

_____

_____

_____

2 How are a "new" Moon and a "full" Moon different?

_____

_____

_____

_____

_____

3 Predict what a clear night with a full Moon might look like.

_____

_____

_____

_____

_____

DO THE ACTIVITY

Working with your research team, carefully follow each step below. Before you start, be sure you know the **safety rules** for this activity.

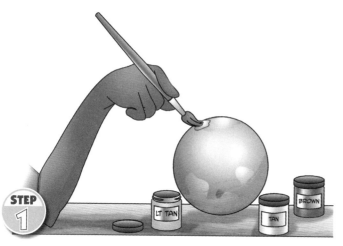

STEP 1

Push the ball gently down onto the dowel rod. **Paint** it to look like the Moon (browns and light tans). **Dry** it overnight. (This will be your moon model.)

STEP 2

Stand about six feet from the lamp (dark room). **Hold** your moon in front of you, slightly above your head (the Earth). Now **face** the "Sun" (lamp).

STEP 3

Slowly **rotate** counter-clockwise, holding your moon in front of you. **Watch** your moon to see how it changes. **Repeat** until everyone has had a turn.

STEP 4

Discuss what happened to your moon. How did the light seem to change your moon's shape? **Compare** your observations with those of other research teams.

WHAT I LEARNED - part 2

Discuss the activity with your team, then answer the questions below.

1 What was moving in this activity? What was not moving?

_____

_____

_____

_____

2 How are the "quarter" Moons similar? How are they different?

_____

_____

_____

_____

3 What might occur if Earth got between the Sun and a full Moon?

_____

_____

_____

_____

SHOW WHAT YOU KNOW - 1

Circle the new Moon with red, first quarter Moon with blue; full Moon with green; and last quarter Moon with yellow. Write the correct names on the lines below.

This is a _____ moon.

_____

This is a _____ moon.

_____

This is a _____ moon.

_____

This is a _____ moon.

_____

To the Parent . . .   **Scripture Connection:** Nehemiah 9:6

Lesson Focus:
Moon Cycles

Lesson Objective:
To explore the relationship between the month and the Moon

National Science Education Standards:
Standard D3 — *"All students should develop an understanding of changes in the Earth and sky . . . objects in the sky have patterns of movement . . . the observable shape of the Moon changes in a cycle that lasts about a month . . ."*

Follow-up Questions:
Ask your child why the Moon appears to change shapes (as it circles the Earth, we see the bright side from different angles).
Ask your child how long it takes for the Moon to circle the Earth (about 30 days or one month).
Ask your child to explain the difference between a "new moon" and a "full moon" (new = all dark; full = all light).

Years & Seasons
Lesson 18

FOCUS Seasons

OBJECTIVE To explore how seasons relate to Earth's movement around the Sun

OVERVIEW A year is equal to one complete trip (revolution) of the Earth around the Sun. During this 12-month cycle, the angle of sunlight hitting the Earth changes, creating weather patterns we call seasons.

WHAT TO DO

With your team, carefully follow each step below.

Observe

Look at the pictures of the seasons on page 120.

Think about how these pictures are different. **Think** about something you might do in each season.

Describe

Describe a day in spring. What would it **look** like? What would it **feel** like? Now **describe** a day for each of the other seasons (summer, fall, winter).

Discuss

What does the Earth revolve around? the Sun

How long does one complete trip take? a year

How long is a year? twelve months

The time periods that we call **years** are based on the movement of the **Earth** around the Sun. Read the story below to find out more.

Years & Seasons

The Earth circles the Sun.

It takes Earth one year (12 months) to circle the Sun. Since the Earth is tilted, the angle of sunlight hitting the Earth changes over time, creating the different seasons.

Earth moves.

One rotation takes 24 hours.

Even though it seems to be sitting still, the Earth is constantly rotating. It takes Earth one **day** to spin around one time.

One revolution takes 12 months.

The Earth is also moving around the Sun. It takes Earth one **year** (12 months) to complete its journey around the Sun.

Earth is tilted.

Earth's tilt affects the angle of sunlight.

As Earth moves around the Sun, the Earth's tilt causes sunlight to hit the Earth at different angles.

Less angle means more warmth.

Summers are warmer than winters because sunlight hits the Earth more directly. Also, the days are much longer in summer.

Seasons change.

The angle changes as Earth moves.

The angle of sunlight gradually changes because Earth is slowly moving around the Sun. This creates the seasons.

The angle creates the seasons.

Only one part of Earth tilts toward the Sun at a time. When it's summer in America, it's winter on the other side of Earth.

WHAT I LEARNED - part 1

Discuss the story with your team, then answer the questions below.

1 Why does the Earth's tilt affect the seasons?

_____

_____

_____

_____

2 Describe how each season is different from the others.

_____

_____

_____

_____

3 How might weather change if Earth wasn't tilted? Why?

_____

_____

_____

_____

DO THE ACTIVITY

Working with your research team, carefully follow each step below. Before you start, be sure you know the **safety rules** for this activity.

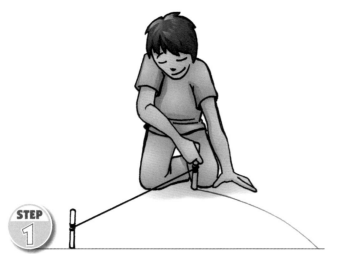

STEP 1

Paint the ball to look like Earth. **Push** the ball gently down onto a dowel rod. Now using the string and chalk, **draw** a 12-foot circle on the pavement.

STEP 2

Divide the circle in half, then **divide** the halves into quarters. Now **divide** the quarters into three equal parts. **Label** each section with a month's name.

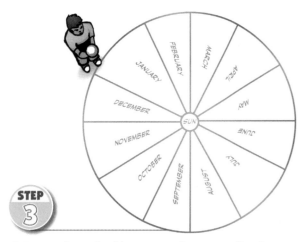

STEP 3

Stand at the edge of January. As you move to the other edge, **rotate** your Earth once for each day in January (31). **Repeat** for each month in the year.

STEP 4

Discuss what this model shows us about Earth's trip around the sun. **Discuss** what it doesn't show us. **Compare** your observations with those of other teams.

WHAT I LEARNED - part 2

Discuss the activity with your team, then answer the questions below.

1 What two ways did your Earth move in this activity?

_____

_____

_____

_____

_____

_____

2 How is January like August? How is it different?

_____

_____

_____

_____

_____

_____

3 What would make this a more accurate model?

_____

_____

_____

_____

_____

SHOW WHAT YOU KNOW - 1

Circle winter with blue. Circle spring with green. Circle summer with brown. Circle fall with orange. Write the correct names on the lines below.

Scene **1** is _____

_ _

Scene **2** is _____

_ _

Scene **3** is _____

_ _

Scene **4** is _____

_ _

To the Parent . . .   **Scripture Connection:** Isaiah 11:6

Lesson Focus:
Seasons

Lesson Objective:
To explore how seasons relate to Earth's movement around the Sun

National Science Education Standards:
Standard D3 — *"All students should develop an understanding of changes in the Earth and sky . . . objects in the sky have patterns of movement . . . changes in the Sun's path create weather patterns that we call the seasons . . ."*

Follow-up Questions:
Ask your child what a year is (a year is one trip of the Earth around the Sun).
Ask your child what causes the seasons (the tilt of the Earth affects sunlight angles. Less angle equals more warmth).
Ask your child to name and describe a season (winter, spring, summer, or fall . . . descriptions will vary).

Physical

LESSONS 19-36

Physical

Energy and Matter

Lessons in this section that start with the "atom girl" focus on the different **states** and unique **properties** of **matter**. You'll discover new things about light and sound. You'll explore physical and chemical reactions. You'll also find out more about electricity and magnetism.

Forces

Lessons in this section that start with the "little hammer" focus on forces. You'll discover how "**push** and **pull**" form the basis for all physical movement. You'll explore simple machines (levers, pulleys). You'll work with Newton's laws of motion. You'll even learn to understand concepts like torque, inertia, and buoyancy.

FOCUS States of Matter

OBJECTIVE To explore Earth's three most common states of matter.

OVERVIEW Everything is made of matter. Matter comes in different forms that scientists call "states." The three most common states on Earth are solid, liquid, and gas.

WHAT TO DO

With your team, carefully follow each step below.

Observe

Look at the antacid tablet. **Look** at the water. **Think** about the three most common states of matter (solid, liquid, gas). Which state describes each item?

Describe

Describe the tablet and the water. What does each one **look** like? What does each one **feel** like? What **color** is each item. What **shape** is each item?

Discuss

What state of matter best describes wood? solid

What state of matter best describes oil? liquid

What state of matter best describes air? gas

The three most common states of matter on Earth are **solid**, **liquid**, and **gas**. Read the story below to find out more about the states of matter.

States of Matter

Everything is made of matter. Matter has different states.

The state of an object's matter determines what the object is like. Matter has three common states on Earth: solid, liquid, and gas. Matter sometimes changes states.

This is a solid.

Sugar is a solid state of matter.

A substance is "solid" when it is firm and has a definite shape. Examples include rocks, wood, glass — or even your lunch!

Dissolving can change the state of sugar.

Mixing sugar with water makes it dissolve. The particles of sugar seem to disappear! The sugar changes from solid to liquid.

This is a liquid.

Water is a liquid state of matter.

A substance is "liquid" when it can flow. Examples include oil, water, or even milk. Some liquids flow easier than others.

Heating can change the state of water.

Heating water makes it boil. When water boils, it turns into a type of gas (steam). The water changes from liquid to gas.

This is a gas.

Propane is a gaseous state of matter.

A substance is a "gas" when it is not a solid or liquid. Examples include air, carbon dioxide, and fuels like propane.

Compression can change the state of gas.

When propane gas is compressed, it turns into a type of liquid. Compressing gas into a liquid makes it easier to transport.

WHAT I LEARNED - part 1

Discuss the story with your team, then answer the questions below.

1 What are the three common states of matter on Earth?

_____

_____

_____

_____

2 How are solids and liquids different?

_____

_____

_____

_____

3 What might happen to a cloud of steam if it suddenly cools?

_____

_____

_____

_____

DO THE ACTIVITY

Working with your research team, carefully follow each step below. Before you start, be sure you know the **safety rules** for this activity.

STEP 1

Examine the antacid tablets, the water, the cup, and the film can. Now **discuss** which state of matter (solid, liquid, or gas) best describes each item.

STEP 2

Fill a clear plastic cup half full of water. **Drop** one antacid tablet into the water. **Watch** the surface of the water and **observe** what happens.

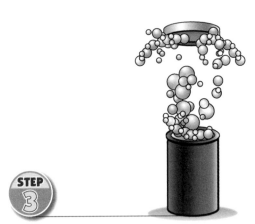

STEP 3

Fill the film can half full of water. **Drop** half an antacid tablet into the water, then quickly **snap on** the lid. **Wait** a few moments and **observe** what happens.

STEP 4

Review steps 2 and 3. **Discuss** which states of matter were present in each step. **Compare** your observations with those of other research teams.

WHAT I LEARNED - part 2

Discuss the activity with your team, then answer the questions below.

1 What states of matter were present in this activity?

_____

_____

_____

_____

_____

_____

2 How were steps 2 and 3 similar? How were they different?

_____

_____

_____

_____

_____

_____

3 If expanding gas couldn't escape, what might happen? Why?

_____

_____

_____

_____

_____

_____

SHOW WHAT YOU KNOW - 1

Circle the **solid** matter in red. Circle the **liquid** matter in blue. Circle the matter that is a **gas** in green. Write the correct "state" on the lines below.

This matter is a

_____

_____

This matter is a

_____

_____

This matter is a

_____

_____

| To the Parent . . . | Scripture Connection: Colossians 3:1-4 |

Lesson Focus:
States of Matter

Lesson Objective:
To explore Earth's three most common states of matter

National Science Education Standards:
Standard B1 — "*All students should understand that materials have observable (and measurable) properties . . . Materials exist in different states . . . some materials can be changed from one state to another . . .*"

Follow-up Questions:
Ask your child to describe the solid state of matter, then give at least one example (rock, wood, ice, etc.).
Ask your child to describe the liquid state of matter, then give at least one example (water, oil, milk, etc.).
Ask your child to describe the gaseous state of matter, then give at least one example (steam, propane, etc.).

FOCUS   Chemical & Physical change

OBJECTIVE   To explore how matter can change from one state to another

OVERVIEW   Matter comes in different forms called "states". But sometimes matter changes from one state to another. Common changes in state are caused by chemical or physical actions.

WHAT TO DO

With your team, carefully follow each step below.

Observe

Look at the baking soda. **Look** at the salt. **Look** at the vinegar. **Think** about what common state of matter (solid, liquid, gas) best describes each item.

Describe

Describe the baking soda, salt, and vinegar. What does each one **look** like? What does each one **feel** like? What does each one **smell** like?

Discuss

What state of matter best describes salt? solid

What state of matter best describes vinegar? liquid

What state of matter best describes air? gas

Matter comes in different states (solid, liquid, gas). But sometimes matter can change from one state to another. Read the story below to find out more.

Changes in Matter

Matter may change from one state to another.
A solid may turn into a liquid. A liquid may turn into a gas. Such changes happen all the time. Common changes in state are caused by chemical or physical actions.

This is a chemical change.

A chemical action may change matter.
There are many kinds of chemical actions like rotting, rusting, and burning. These actions make different substances.

For instance, mixing baking soda (sodium bicarbonate) with vinegar (acetic acid) creates carbon dioxide (CO_2). The *solid* and the *liquid* combine to make a *gas*.

This is a physical change.

A physical action may change matter.
There are many kinds of physical actions like cutting, melting, freezing, or boiling. These can make matter change states.

Boiling can create physical change.
Heating water makes it boil. When water boils, it turns into a type of gas (steam). The matter changes from liquid to gas.

Changes happen all the time.

Changes in matter can be natural.
Unprotected iron rusts over time (chemical change). Cold weather can turn liquid water to solid ice (physical change).

Changes can also be caused by people.
Scientists combine chemicals and other ingredients to create many useful items — from plastic spoons to airplane parts!

WHAT I LEARNED - part 1

Discuss the story with your team, then answer the questions below.

1 Name two types of change that may affect matter's state.

_____

_____

_____

_____

_____

_____

2 How are freezing and boiling similar? How are they different?

_____

_____

_____

_____

_____

_____

3 What are some ways you could change the state of water?

_____

_____

_____

_____

_____

_____

DO THE ACTIVITY

Working with your research team, carefully follow each step below. Before you start, be sure you know the **safety rules** for this activity.

STEP 1

Examine the salt, baking soda, and vinegar. **Discuss** which state of matter (solid, liquid, or gas) best describes each item. **Pour** a little salt into one balloon.

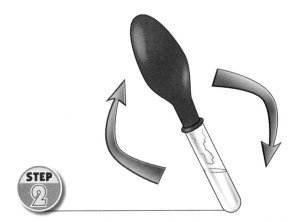

STEP 2

Pour an inch of vinegar into the tube. **Attach** the balloon to the top of the tube. Now quickly **tip** the balloon so the salt falls in the tube. **Observe** what happens.

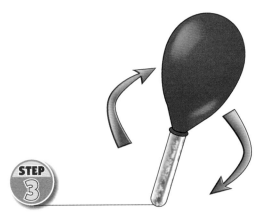

STEP 3

Empty the tube and **rinse** with clean water. Now **pour** a little baking soda in the other balloon. **Repeat** step 2. Carefully **observe** what happens.

STEP 4

Compare steps 2 and 3. **Discuss** what states of matter were shown in each step. **Compare** your observations with those of other research teams.

WHAT I LEARNED - part 2

Discuss the activity with your team, then answer the questions below.

1 What states of matter were demonstrated? How?

_____

_____

_____

_____

_____

_____

2 How were steps 2 and 3 similar? How were they different?

_____

_____

_____

_____

_____

_____

3 How might baking soda help bread dough rise?

_____

_____

_____

_____

_____

_____

SHOW WHAT YOU KNOW - 1

Circle any **physical** change in red. Circle any **chemical** change in blue. Write the word that best describes the change on the lines below.

These changes are

_____

_ _ _ _ _ _ _ _ _ _ _ _ _ _

_____

These changes are

_____

_ _ _ _ _ _ _ _ _ _ _ _ _ _

_____

To the Parent . . .   **Scripture Connection:** I Corinthians 15:52

Lesson Focus:
Chemical and Physical Change

Lesson Objective:
To explore how matter can change from one state to another

National Science Education Standards:
Standard B1 — *"All students should understand that materials have observable (and measurable) properties . . .*
Materials exist in different states . . . some materials can be changed from one state to another . . ."

Follow-up Questions:
Ask your child to name the three most common states of matter on Earth (solid, liquid, gas).
Ask your child to describe a physical change in matter, then give an example (water turns to ice, water turns to steam, etc.).
Ask your child to describe a chemical change in matter, then give an example (baking soda and vinegar make a gas, etc.).

Bubble Bonds
Lesson 21

FOCUS Bonds

OBJECTIVE To explore how the bonds between atoms hold things together

OVERVIEW Atoms are tiny particles of matter. Atoms can link together. Scientists call this link a "bond." The stronger the bond, the stronger the material.

WHAT TO DO

With your team, carefully follow each step below.

Observe

Look at the bubble solution. **Think** about what it is made from (water and liquid soap). How is this material like other liquids you have seen? How is it different?

Describe

Describe the bubble solution. What does it **look** like? What **color** is it? What does it **smell** like? What does it **feel** like? How is it different from bottled water?

Discuss

What is one tiny particle of matter called? atom

What word means "to link things together"? bond

What is a mix of different liquids called? solution

Atoms are tiny particles of matter. Atoms can link together to create a **bond**. Read the story below to find out more about bonds.

Atoms & Bonds

Atoms link together to form bonds.

An atom is a tiny particle of matter. It is far too small to see. Everything is made from atoms. Atoms can link together. Scientists call this link a "bond."

Liquids have bonds.

Water is held together by bonds.

The atoms in water link together to form surface tension. This is a very weak kind of bond. Otherwise we could walk on water!

Soap is held together by bonds.

Blow air into soap and its bonds hold it together as bubbles. Soap's bonds are stronger than water's, but still break easily.

Solids have bonds.

Wood is held together by bonds.

Wood atoms have strong bonds. Steel atoms have even stronger bonds! The stronger the bond, the stronger the material.

Bonds make materials useful.

Different materials like soap, water, wood, metal, plastic, or glass are used in different ways because of their bonds.

Bonds can be broken.

Physical actions break bonds.

Bonds can be broken by physical actions. Sawing a board, boiling water, and melting steel are good examples.

Chemical actions break bonds.

Bonds can be broken by chemical actions. When you eat an apple, chemicals break it into the nutrients your body needs.

WHAT I LEARNED - part 1

Discuss the story with your team, then answer the questions below.

1 Why is it easy to break a soap bubble?

_____

_____

_____

_____

_____

2 Why is a plastic knife stronger than a paper towel?

_____

_____

_____

_____

_____

3 Which would you use to wrap presents - paper or steel? Why?

_____

_____

_____

_____

_____

DO THE ACTIVITY

Working with your research team, carefully follow each step below. Before you start, be sure you know the **safety rules** for this activity.

STEP 1

Look at the bubble solution in your petri dish. **Place** the end of the largest straw into the solution. **Blow** through the straw gently. **Observe** what happens.

STEP 2

Repeat step 1 using the medium straw. **Observe** any changes in the bubbles. **Repeat** again using the small straw. **Observe** what happens.

STEP 3

Gently **insert** the small straw into the large bubble. **Blow** gently. Try to make a small bubble inside the large bubble. **Observe** what happens.

STEP 4

Review each step. **Discuss** how bubbles are made and what holds them together. **Compare** your findings with those of other research teams.

WHAT I LEARNED - part 2

Discuss the activity with your team, then answer the questions below.

1 What was different between step 1 and step 2?

_____

_____

_____

_____

_____

2 How were the straws similar? How were they different?

_____

_____

_____

_____

_____

3 How would step 1 change if you only used water? Why?

_____

_____

_____

_____

_____

NAME _____

SHOW WHAT YOU KNOW - 1

Atoms can link together to create a bond. Write the correct word on each line below. Now circle the object in each pair that has the strongest bonds.

_____ are tiny particles of matter.   _____ means "to link together."

_____   _____

1.

2.

3.
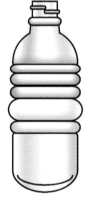

4.

To the Parent . . .   **Scripture Connection:** Colossians 3:13-14

Lesson Focus:
Bonds

Lesson Objective:
To explore how bonds between atoms hold things together

National Science Education Standards:
Standard B1 — *"All students should develop an understanding (that) . . . objects are made of one or more materials such as paper, wood, or metal. Objects can be described by the properties of the materials from which they are made . . ."*

Follow-up Questions:
Ask your child to explain what an "atom" is (a tiny particle of matter that is too small to see).
Ask your child what scientists call it when atoms link together (a bond).
Ask your child how bonds can be broken (physical actions like sawing wood; chemical actions like digesting food).

FOCUS Surface Tension

OBJECTIVE To explore the concept of surface tension

OVERVIEW Surface tension happens because water molecules stick to each other. Scientists call connections like this a "bond." But when a bond is broken, interesting things can happen!

WHAT TO DO

With your team, carefully follow each step below.

Observe

Look at the soap, water, and paper. **Think** about the three most common states of matter on Earth (solid, liquid, gas). Which state describes each item?

Describe

Describe the water and the soap. What does each one **look** like? What does each one **feel** like? How are they **similar**? How are they **different**?

Discuss

What word means "to stick to each other"? bond

What word is "a tiny piece of matter"? molecule

Where might you find "surface tension"? water

Surface tension happens when water molecules cling to each other. But surface tension is easily broken. Read the story below to find out more.

Surface Tension

Surface tension happens when molecules stick together.

Molecules are tiny pieces of matter. Some molecules cling to each other, especially at the top of liquids. Scientists call this "surface tension." Surface tension is a weak bond.

This is water.

Water molecules cling together.

Water molecules pull toward each other and cling together. Even a glass of water has a little tension on its surface.

Clinging molecules create surface tension.

Surface tension pulls constantly. Its force causes small bits of water to form into "drops" instead of spreading out.

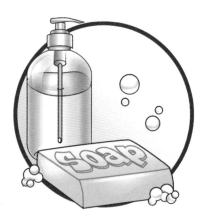

This is soap.

Soap can break surface tension.

Some substances, like soaps, can break the weak bond between water molecules. This breaks surface tension.

Soap makes cleaning easier.

By breaking surface tension, soap makes it easier for water molecules to attach to dirt and wash it away.

This is a mayfly.

Mayflies use surface tension.

Mayflies are very light insects. Surface tension is just strong enough to let mayflies land on top of the water.

Surface tension holds mayflies up.

Mayflies don't float like boats do. If surface tension were suddenly gone, then the mayfly would sink!

WHAT I LEARNED - part 1

Discuss the story with your team, then answer the questions below.

1 What makes small bits of water form into drops?

_____
_____
_____
_____
_____

2 Which washes dishes better — soapy water or plain? Why?

_____
_____
_____
_____
_____

3 What might happen to a mayfly if soap got in its pond?

_____
_____
_____
_____

DO THE ACTIVITY

Working with your research team, carefully follow each step below. Before you start, be sure you know the **safety rules** for this activity.

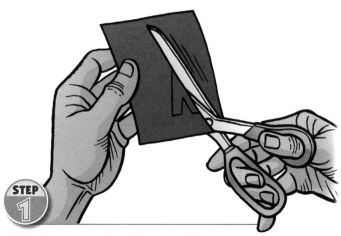

STEP 1

Fill the petri dish with water. **Place** a drop of liquid soap on the wax paper. Now **cut out** the two boat shapes from the sheet of paper your teacher gives you.

STEP 2

Carefully **place** the first boat on the water. **Touch** the tip of the toothpick to the water in the center of the notch. **Observe** what happens. **Remove** the boat.

STEP 3

Carefully **place** the second boat in the water. **Dip** the toothpick in the liquid soap. **Stick** the tip of the soapy toothpick in the notch again. **Observe** what happens.

STEP 4

Review steps 2 and 3. **Discuss** how they were similar and how they were different. **Compare** your observations with those of other research teams.

WHAT I LEARNED - part 2

Discuss the activity with your team, then answer the questions below.

1 What did the boat do in step 2? What did it do in step 3?

_____

_____

_____

_____

_____

_____

2 What made the liquid different in step 3? What changed?

_____

_____

_____

_____

_____

_____

3 What other kinds of "bonds" have you seen? Give examples.

_____

_____

_____

_____

_____

SHOW WHAT YOU KNOW - 1

Show what you know about **surface tension**. Circle the correct answers to each question. (Note: Some of the questions have more than one right answer!)

Which pictures are good illustrations of surface tension?

Which object can stay on top of the water without floating?

Which makes cleaning easier by breaking surface tension?

To the Parent . . .   **Scripture Connection:** Ephesians 4:2-3

Lesson Focus:
Surface Tension

Lesson Objective:
To explore the concept of surface tension

National Science Education Standards:
Standard B1 — *"All students should understand that materials have observable (and measureable) properties . . . Materials exist in different states . . . some materials can be changed from one state to another . . ."*

Follow-up Questions:
Ask your child how surface tension makes water into drops (causes water molecules to cling together, pull closer).
Ask your child how some insects can use surface tension (can stay on top of the water without floating.).
Ask your child how soap can make cleaning easier (breaks surface tension).

FOCUS Properties of Matter

OBJECTIVE To explore how mixing two colors can make a third color

OVERVIEW Every material is different. We can see something's size or color. We can feel its weight or its temperature. Scientists call these "properties." A material's properties determine how it affects other materials.

WHAT TO DO

With your team, carefully follow each step below.

Observe

Look at the white milk, the blue food coloring, and the yellow food coloring. **Think** about what these three things have in common.

Describe

Describe all three liquids. What does each one **look** like? What **color** is each one? How are they **similar**? How are they **different**?

Discuss

What makes materials different? properties

How is a baseball different from a softball? size

How are glass and paper cups different? weight

Every kind of material is different. Scientists call these differences **properties**. Read the story below to find out more about properties.

Different Things

Materials are different in many ways.

Differences can include size, color, weight, or even temperature. Scientists call these differences "properties." Properties determine how materials affect other materials.

Toys can be different.

A bowling ball is heavy and hard.

A bowling ball's properties make it perfect for bowling. But imagine using a bowling ball to play volleyball. Ouch!

A pool toy is large and light.

The properties of a pool toy make it great for floating on the water. But a pool toy wouldn't work at all to build a treehouse.

Food can be different.

Peanuts come in many forms.

Roasted peanuts are hard and crunchy. Boiled peanuts are soft like peas. Ground up peanuts make sticky peanut butter.

Peanuts can be used in many ways.

The properties of peanuts make them useful in making paint, soap, plastics, bug sprays, and even some cosmetics!

Color can be different.

Color is one kind of property.

Color tells us many things. A yellow banana tastes different from a brown one. A black shirt gets hotter than a white one in the sun

Properties have properties, too!

A color can be light or dark. A color can have different shades. When colors are mixed together, they can make other colors.

WHAT I LEARNED - part 1

Discuss the story with your team, then answer the questions below.

1 List some properties that materials might have.

_____

_____

_____

_____

_____

_____

2 Name two kinds of balls and tell how they are different.

_____

_____

_____

_____

_____

_____

3 What are some properties of snow? How might these change?

_____

_____

_____

_____

_____

_____

DO THE ACTIVITY

Working with your research team, carefully follow each step below. Before you start, be sure you know the **safety rules** for this activity.

STEP 1

Place the petri dish on a paper towel. **Fill** the petri dish with milk. Carefully **place** one drop of blue food coloring in the middle of the dish.

STEP 2

Now carefully **place** one drop of yellow food coloring about 1 inch away from the spot of blue food coloring. (An inch is about the width of your thumb.)

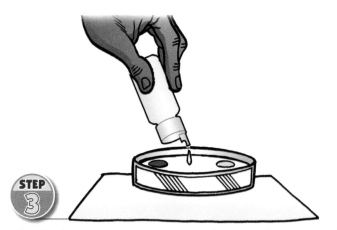

STEP 3

Quicky **add** one or two drops of liquid soap between the two spots of color. **Observe** what happens as the soap changes the properties of the milk.

STEP 4

Review the steps in this activity. **Discuss** what caused the colors to mix together. **Compare** your observations with those of other research teams.

WHAT I LEARNED - part 2

Discuss the activity with your team, then answer the questions below.

1 What happens when blue and yellow are mixed together?

_____

_____

_____

_____

_____

2 How were steps 2 and 3 similar? How were they different?

_____

_____

_____

_____

_____

3 How might water's properties change if you froze it?

_____

_____

_____

_____

_____

SHOW WHAT YOU KNOW - 1

Look at the materials below. Draw a line from each material to what it might look like if one of its **properties** changed. Fill in the blank with the correct word.

Row 1

Row 2

Every material has different

_____

To the Parent . . .   **Scripture Connection:** Psalms 139:14

Lesson Focus:
Properties of Matter

Lesson Objective:
To explore how mixing two colors can make a third color

National Science Education Standards:
Standard B1 — *"All students should understand that materials have observable properties . . . including size, weight, shape, color, temperature, and the ability to react with other substances . . ."*

Follow-up Questions:
Every material is different. Ask your child what scientists call these differences (properties).
Ask your child to list some properties that materials might have (size, weight, shape, color, temperature, etc.).
Ask your child how freezing water changes its properties (makes it hard, makes it colder, etc.).

Little Lava-Lamp
Lesson 24

FOCUS — Density

OBJECTIVE — To explore how density affects matter

OVERVIEW — "Density" means how tightly molecules are packed together. (Molecules are the tiny particles everything is made from.) An object's density can determine how its matter behaves, or even how its matter affects other matter.

WHAT TO DO

With your team, carefully follow each step below.

Observe

Look at the **tablet**, the **water**, and the **oil**. **Think** about the three most common states of matter on Earth (solid, liquid, gas). Which state describes each item?

Describe

Describe the **water** and the **oil**. What does each one **look** like? What does each one **feel** like? How are they similar? How are they different?

Discuss

What state of matter is the tint tablet? solid

What state of matter is the water or oil? liquid

What state of matter best describes a bubble? gas

Every kind of matter has a certain **density**. Density means how tightly **molecules** are packed together. Read the story below to find out more.

Density

Everything on Earth has a certain density.

Density is a word scientists use to tell how tightly molecules are packed together. Things that are more dense are heavier. Things that are less dense are lighter.

This is iron

Iron is matter in a solid state.

A solid is usually more dense than a liquid or gas. Iron molecules are more tightly packed together than water or air molecules.

Solids can have different density.

Iron is very dense. Foam is not very dense. A piece of iron is much heavier than the same size piece of foam.

This is water.

Water is matter in a liquid state.

Liquids are usually less dense than solids, but more dense than gases. This makes water lighter than iron, but heavier than air.

Liquids can have different density.

If the density of two liquids is different, they may not mix together. The lighter liquid will usually float to the top.

This is air.

Air is matter in a gaseous state.

Gases are usually less dense than solids or liquids. When air is released in water, it forms a bubble and rises to the surface.

Air can have different density.

Cold air is more dense than hot air. The warmest air in a room will be at the ceiling. Air density can even affect weather.

WHAT I LEARNED - part 1

Discuss the story with your team, then answer the questions below.

1 What makes an object a certain density?

_____

_____

_____

_____

_____

2 How are cold air and hot air similar? How are they different?

_____

_____

_____

_____

_____

3 Oil is less dense than water. What does oil do if poured in water?

_____

_____

_____

_____

_____

DO THE ACTIVITY

Working with your research team, carefully follow each step below. Before you start, be sure you know the **safety rules** for this activity.

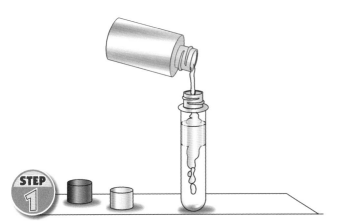

STEP 1

Fill the tube half full of water. Now slowly **add** oil until the tube is full. **Hold** the tube very still until the two liquids have completely stopped moving.

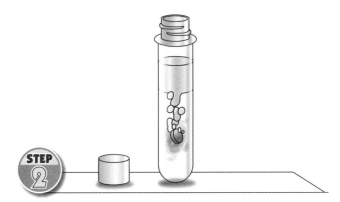

STEP 2

Drop the tint tablet into the tube. Carefully **observe** what happens. At what point did the tablet begin to dissolve? **Discuss** what you see happening.

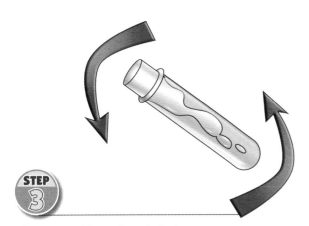

STEP 3

Once the bubbles are gone, **fasten** the lid on the tube. Slowly **turn** it upside down. (Do not shake!) **Observe** what happens. **Repeat** until everyone has had a turn.

STEP 4

Review each step in this activity. **Discuss** the states of matter present in each step. **Compare** your observations with those of other teams.

WHAT I LEARNED - part 2

Discuss the activity with your team, then answer the questions below.

1 What did the tint tablet do in oil? What did it do in water?

_____

_____

_____

_____

_____

_____

2 Which is more dense — water or oil? How could you tell?

_____

_____

_____

_____

_____

_____

3 If you dropped a BB in the tube, where would it go? Why?

_____

_____

_____

_____

_____

_____

SHOW WHAT YOU KNOW - 1

Circle the **solid** matter in red. Circle the **liquid** matter in blue. Circle the matter that is a **gas** in green. Write the correct "state" on the lines below.

The least dense matter is

_____

_ _ _ _ _ _ _ _ _ _ _ _ _ _ _ _ _ _ _ _

The most dense matter is

_____

_ _ _ _ _ _ _ _ _ _ _ _ _ _ _ _ _ _ _ _

The medium dense matter is

_____

_ _ _ _ _ _ _ _ _ _ _ _ _ _ _ _ _ _ _ _

To the Parent . . .   **Scripture Connection:** Job 37:16

Lesson Focus:
Density

Lesson Objective:
To explore how density affects matter

National Science Education Standards:
Standard B1 — *"All students should understand that materials have observable (and measurable) properties . . .*
Materials exist in different states . . . some materials can be changed from one state to another . . ."

Follow-up Questions:
Ask your child which state of matter is the most dense (solid). Ask for an example of a solid.
Ask your child which state of matter is the least dense (gas). Ask for an example of a gas.
Ask your child to give an example of how density affects matter (oil floats on water; bubbles rise to surface; etc.).

Spoonful of Sound
Lesson 25

FOCUS   Sound

OBJECTIVE   To explore how sound is created by vibration

OVERVIEW   Vibration is when an object moves back and forth very rapidly. When this movement makes a noise we can hear, we call it "sound."

WHAT TO DO

With your team, carefully follow each step below.

Observe

Look at the three spoons. **Think** about how these spoons are similar. **Think** about how these spoons are different. **Discuss** what each spoon might be used for.

Describe

Describe each spoon. What does it **look** like? What does it **feel** like? What **color** is it? What **shape** is it? How is each spoon **different** from the others?

Discuss

What is the hardest spoon made from? metal

What is the white spoon made from? plastic

What is the odd-shaped spoon made from? wood

Vibration is a rapid back and forth movement. If this movement makes a noise we can hear, we call it "**sound**." Read the story below to find out more.

Sound

All sound is caused by vibration.

Vibration is a rapid back and forth movement. Different vibrations produce different sounds. Musical instruments use different kinds of vibrations to make music.

This is a drum.

A drum makes sound through vibration.

When you bang on a drum, its surface (or "skin") vibrates. This vibration makes a sound that is unique to that kind of drum.

Different drums make different sounds.

The sound an object makes can be affected by its size, its shape, or the material that it is made from.

This is a guitar.

A guitar makes sound through vibration.

When you pluck a guitar's strings, they vibrate. If the string is shorter, the sound is higher. If it is longer, the sound is lower.

The player controls the vibration.

By moving his fingers, a guitarist can make a string longer or shorter. This changes the vibration, which changes the sound.

This is a trumpet.

A trumpet makes sound through vibration.

When you blow a trumpet, your lips vibrate against the mouth-piece. The vibration goes through the horn, making a sound.

Different horns make different sounds.

The sound a horn makes can be affected by the horn's size, its shape, or the material the horn is made from.

WHAT I LEARNED - part 1

Discuss the story with your team, then answer the questions below.

1 What is vibration? What is the noise it can create called?

_____

_____

_____

_____

_____

2 How are a trumpet and drum similar? How are they different?

_____

_____

_____

_____

_____

3 What might happen if a drum's skin became loose? Why?

_____

_____

_____

_____

_____

DO THE ACTIVITY

Working with your research team, carefully follow each step below. Before you start, be sure you know the **safety rules** for this activity.

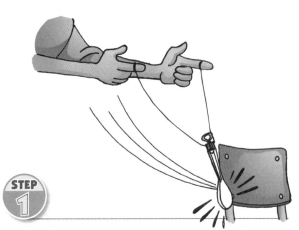

STEP 1

Clip the center of the string to the end of a spoon. **Wrap** the ends of the string around your index fingers. **Tap** the spoon on a chair. **Record** what you hear.

STEP 2

Place your index fingers in your ears. Tap the spoon on a chair again. **Record** what you hear. **Compare** this to the sound you heard in step 1.

STEP 3

Repeat steps 1 and 2 using the other two spoons. **Record** what you hear with each change. Make sure everyone on your team has a turn.

STEP 4

Compare all the sounds you heard in this activity. **Discuss** your observations with your team, then **compare** findings with other research teams.

WHAT I LEARNED - part 2

Discuss the activity with your team, then answer the questions below.

1 Describe each spoon. What was each one made from?

_____

_____

_____

_____

2 How were the spoons' sounds similar? How were they different?

_____

_____

_____

_____

_____

3 Would all metal spoons sound the same? Why or why not?

_____

_____

_____

_____

NAME _____

SHOW WHAT YOU KNOW - 1

Sound is created by vibration. Circle in red the objects that vibrate easily to create sounds. Write the correct word on the line below.

Every sound is created by a

_____

_____

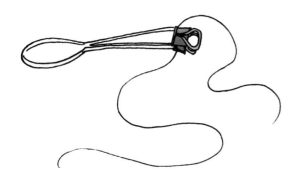

To the Parent . . .   **Scripture Connection:** I Chronicles 15:28

Lesson Focus:
Sound

Lesson Objective:
To explore how sound is created by vibration

National Science Education Standards:
Standard B2 — *"All students should develop an understanding of position and motion of objects . . . (both) can be changed by pushing or pulling . . . sound is produced by vibrating objects . . . pitch can be varied by changing rate of vibration . . ."*

Follow-up Questions:
Ask your child what causes sound (vibration).
Ask your child what the word "vibration" means (rapid back and forth movement).
Ask your child to name at least one thing that might affect a musical instrument's sound (size, shape, or materials).

String-Thing
Lesson 26

FOCUS   Pitch

OBJECTIVE   To explore how changing the rate of vibration changes the sound

OVERVIEW   Sounds are created by vibration. If the rate of vibration changes, then the pitch (tone) of the sound changes, too.

WHAT TO DO

With your team, carefully follow each step below.

Observe

Hold the string in your hand. **Look** at the string closely.

Now **ask** a team member to stretch the string tightly.

Pluck the string and **listen** to the result.

Describe

Describe the string. What does it **look** like? What does it **feel** like? What can you do to make the string make a sound? What might **change** the sound?

Discuss

What do we call noise we can hear?   sound

What is it that creates sound?   vibration

What are changes in sound called?   pitch

READ THE STORY

Vibration creates sound. If the rate of vibration changes, then the sound changes, too. Read the story below to find out more.

Changes in Sound

Different vibrations create different sounds.

Vibration is a rapid back and forth movement. If the speed of the vibration changes, then the sound changes, too. The tone a sound makes is called its "pitch."

These are handbells.

Handbells make sound through vibration.

When you ring a handbell, a clapper strikes the shell of the bell, making it vibrate. We hear this vibration as sound.

Different bells have different sounds.

A bell's sound is determined by its size and shape. Every bell is designed to play only one very specific pitch.

This is a violin.

A violin makes sound through vibration.

The bow vibrates the violin's strings. The tighter the string, the faster it vibrates. The faster it vibrates, the higher the pitch.

Changing vibration changes pitch.

By moving his fingers, a musician can tighten or loosen a string. This changes the vibration, which changes the pitch.

This is your voice.

People make sound through vibration.

Your throat contains "vocal chords." When you speak, air passes through your vocal chords, making them vibrate.

Changing vocal chords changes pitch.

If you tighten your vocal chords, the pitch is higher. If you loosen your vocal chords, the pitch is lower.

WHAT I LEARNED - part 1

Discuss the story with your team, then answer the questions below.

1 What causes sound to change? What is pitch?

_____

_____

_____

_____

_____

2 How are vocal chords like violin strings? How are they different?

_____

_____

_____

_____

_____

_____

3 When someone is frightened, their vocal chords tighten. How might this affect their voice? Explain your answer.

_____

_____

_____

_____

_____

DO THE ACTIVITY

Working with your research team, carefully follow each step below. Before you start, be sure you know the **safety rules** for this activity.

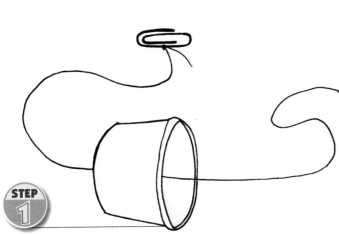

STEP 1

Tie the paperclip to the end of the string. **Slide** the knot to the center of the paperclip. **Push** the other end of the string through the hole in the bottom of the cup.

STEP 2

Pull the string until the paperclip rests on the bottom of the cup. **Ask** a team member to hold the cup firmly, then **pull** the string until it is tight.

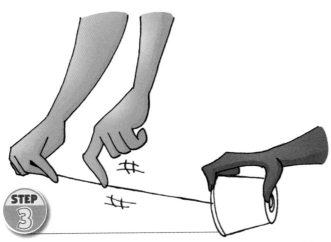

STEP 3

Pluck the string and listen to the result. Now **loosen** or **tighten** the string and repeat. **Compare** the sounds the string makes as you loosen and tighten the string.

STEP 4

The tighter the string, the faster it vibrated. **Discuss** the effect this had on the sound, then **compare** your team's findings with other research teams.

WHAT I LEARNED - part 2

Discuss the activity with your team, then answer the questions below.

1 Did tightening the string make pitch go up or down? Why?

_____

_____

_____

_____

_____

2 How was your "string thing" like a guitar? How was it different?

_____

_____

_____

_____

_____

3 If the string is too loose, what happens to the sound? Why?

_____

_____

_____

_____

_____

SHOW WHAT YOU KNOW - 1

Vibration creates **sound**. The rate of vibration changes the **pitch**. Circle the objects that can change their pitch easily. Write the correct word on the line below.

Vibration rate changes the

_____

_____

To the Parent . . .   **Scripture Connection:** Proverbs 15:1

Lesson Focus:
Pitch (or tone)

Lesson Objective:
To explore how changing the rate of vibration changes pitch

National Science Education Standards:
Standard B2 — *"All students should develop an understanding of position and motion of objects . . . (both) can be changed by pushing or pulling . . . sound is produced by vibrating objects . . . pitch can be varied by changing rate of vibration . . ."*

Follow-up Questions:
Ask your child what causes sound (vibration). Ask your child to describe some common sounds.
Ask your child what changes in vibration are called (pitch).
Ask your child what causes pitch to go up or down as we speak (vocal chords get tighter or looser).

FOCUS   Sound and Density

OBJECTIVE   To explore how density affects the speed of sound

OVERVIEW   Sound can travel at different speeds depending on what it's traveling through. Generally, the denser the substance (the closer its molecules), the faster sound can travel.

WHAT TO DO

With your team, carefully follow each step below.

Observe

Look at the two balloons. **Think** about how they are similar. **Think** about how they are different. **Discuss** some things that balloons might be used for.

Describe

Describe each balloon. What does it **look** like? What does it **feel** like? What **color** is it? What are some ways you might **change** a balloon's shape?

Discuss

What substance will be inside Balloon 1? air

What substance will be inside Balloon 2? water

What word means "closer molecules"? dense

READ THE STORY

Sound travels at different speeds depending on what kind of substance it's traveling through. Read the story below to find out more.

The Speed of Sound

Sound can travel at different speeds.

Sound travels at different speeds depending on what it's traveling through. Generally the denser the substance (the closer its molecules are), the faster sound can travel.

Sounds are slow in gases.

Air is a gas. It is not very dense.

Vibration causes molecules to "bump together," making sound. Since air molecules are far apart, sound is slower through air.

Sound travels slowly through air.

Sound travels through the air at about 750 miles per hour. The temperature of air can affect sound speeds slightly.

Sounds are faster in liquids.

Water is a liquid. It is much denser than air.

Molecules in liquids are closer together than those in gases. This allows sound to travel much faster through water than air.

Sound travels faster through water.

Sound travels through water at about 3,300 miles per hour. This lets some sea creatures communicate over long distances.

Sounds are fastest in solids.

Copper is a solid. It is much denser than water.

The particles in solids like copper are very tightly packed. This allows the vibrations that create sound to travel very rapidly.

Sound travels very fast through copper.

Sound travels through copper at about 13,000 miles per hour. Copper wire is used to transfer audio signals (a form of sound).

WHAT I LEARNED - part 1

Discuss the story with your team, then answer the questions below.

1 Why is sound slower in air than water?

_____

_____

_____

_____

_____

_____

2 How are copper and cotton similar? How are they different?

_____

_____

_____

_____

_____

_____

3 Would sound be faster through steel or grape juice? Why?

_____

_____

_____

_____

_____

DO THE ACTIVITY

Working with your research team, carefully follow each step below. Before you start, be sure you know the **safety rules** for this activity.

STEP 1

Scratch the pencil eraser with a fingernail. **Record** what you hear. **Hold** the pencil in your teeth and **scratch** it again. **Compare** this to the first sound.

STEP 2

Fill Balloon 1 with air. **Tie** it shut. **Fill** Balloon 2 with water. **Tie** it shut. **Place** Balloon 1 against your ear. **Tap** it lightly with the pencil. **Record** what you hear.

STEP 3

Place Balloon 2 against your ear. **Tap** it lightly with the pencil. **Compare** the sound you hear to Balloon 1. Make sure everyone on your team has a turn.

STEP 4

Compare all the sounds you heard in this activity. **Discuss** your observations with your team, then **compare** findings with other research teams.

WHAT I LEARNED - part 2

Discuss the activity with your team, then answer the questions below.

1 Which balloon allowed the sound to travel better? Why?

_____

_____

_____

_____

_____

2 How were the two balloons similar? How were they different?

_____

_____

_____

_____

_____

3 Which might hear sounds farther — a dolphin or dog? Why?

_____

_____

_____

_____

_____

SHOW WHAT YOU KNOW - 1

Sound travels at different speeds through a solid, a liquid, or a gas. Circle the objects to show how fast sound travels. Use red for slow, blue for faster, green for fastest. Write the correct word on the lines below.

The least dense matter is

_ _ _ _ _ _ _ _ _ _ _ _ _ _ _ _

The most dense matter is

_ _ _ _ _ _ _ _ _ _ _ _ _ _ _ _

The medium dense matter is

_ _ _ _ _ _ _ _ _ _ _ _ _ _ _ _

To the Parent . . .   **Scripture Connection:** I Peter 1:14

Lesson Focus:
Sound and Density

Lesson Objective:
To explore how density affects the transfer of sound

National Science Education Standards:
Standard B2 — *"All students should develop an understanding of position and motion of objects . . . (both) can be changed by pushing or pulling . . . sound is produced by vibrating objects . . . pitch can be varied by changing rate of vibration . . ."*

Follow-up Questions:
Ask your child to name one thing that can affect the speed of sound (the substance the sound is traveling through).
Ask your child to compare sound speeds through a gas, a liquid, and a solid (gas = slow, liquid = faster, solid = fastest).
Ask your child why sound travels faster through water than air (water is more dense; its molecules are closer together).

Newton's Third
Lesson 28

FOCUS Action/Reaction

OBJECTIVE To understand Newton's third law of motion

OVERVIEW Forces always come in pairs. When an object pushes (or pulls) another object, the second object reacts with equal force in the opposite direction.

WHAT TO DO

With your team, carefully follow each step below.

Observe

Look at the pictures on page 178. **Talk** about how these things are different from each other. Now **discuss** some ways that these things might be similar.

Describe

Describe each thing on page 178. What does it **look** like? What might it **feel** like? What **color** is it? What **shape** is it? What is it doing?

Discuss

Where might you see birds moving fast? air

Where might you see fish moving fast? water

Where might you see cars moving fast? road

Newton's third law says, "For every action, there is an equal and opposite reaction." Read the story below to find out what this means.

Newton's Third Law

For every action, there is an equal and opposite reaction.
Forces always come in pairs. When an object pushes (or pulls) another object, the second object reacts with equal force in the opposite direction.

Birds use action/reaction.

A bird's wings push the air down.
When a bird beats its wings, the action pushes air downward. When the air goes down, something else must go up!

The reaction pushes the bird up.
The downward force on the air creates an upward force on the bird. This reaction helps birds climb high into the sky.

Fish use action/reaction.

A fish's fins push the water backward.
When a fish flips its fins, the action pushes water backward. When the water goes back, something else must go forward.

The reaction pushes the fish forward.
The backward force on the water creates a forward force on the fish. This reaction helps fish swim rapidly through the sea.

Cars use action/reaction.

A car's wheels push the road backward.
As a car's wheels turn, they push backward against the road. A backward push means something else must go forward.

The reaction pushes the car forward.
The backward force on the road creates a forward force on the car. This reaction can help cars go very fast.

WHAT I LEARNED - part 1

Discuss the story with your team, then answer the questions below.

1 What is Newton's third law? Give one example.

_____

_____

_____

_____

_____

_____

2 How are fish and bird movements similar? How do they differ?

_____

_____

_____

_____

_____

_____

3 If a car's wheels push forward, what is the car's reaction?

_____

_____

_____

_____

_____

_____

DO THE ACTIVITY

Working with your research team, carefully follow each step below. Before you start, be sure you know the **safety rules** for this activity.

STEP 1

Inflate and **tie** Balloon 1. **Tape** the straw parallel to the balloon. **Run** the string through the straw, then **hold** the ends of the string and **stretch** it tight.

STEP 2

Blow Balloon 1 from one end of the string to the other. **Time** how long it takes. Now **repeat** step 1 with Balloon 2, but don't tie the end! (Just **hold** it shut for now.)

STEP 3

Release the end of Balloon 2. **Time** how long it takes to reach the end of the string. **Compare** this to Balloon 1's trip. **Repeat** if desired.

STEP 4

Review the different ballon trips. **Discuss** your observations with your team, then **compare** your findings with those of other research teams.

WHAT I LEARNED - part 2

Discuss the activity with your team, then answer the questions below.

1 Which balloon created more action? Which went fastest?

_____

_____

_____

_____

_____

2 How were the balloon trips similar? How were they different?

_____

_____

_____

_____

_____

3 How might a larger balloon change the trip? Why?

_____

_____

_____

_____

_____

SHOW WHAT YOU KNOW - 1

Newton's third law says, "For every **action**, there is an equal and opposite **reaction**." Look at the pictures below, then write the correct word on each line.

fins flap back ◄······   ······► fish goes forward

_____   _____

_____   _____

wings beat down   bird goes up

_____   _____

_____   _____

wheels push back ◄······   ······► car goes forward

_____   _____

_____   _____

To the Parent . . .   **Scripture Connection:** Proverbs 15:13

Lesson Focus:
Action / Reaction

Lesson Objective:
To understand Newton's third law of motion

National Science Education Standards:
Standard B2 — *"All students should develop an understanding of position and motion of objects . . . (both) can be changed by pushing or pulling . . . sound is produced by vibrating objects . . . pitch can be varied by changing rate of vibration . . ."*

Follow-up Questions:
Ask your child, "What do forces always come in?" (pairs).
Ask your child to explain Newton's third law of motion (for every action, there is an equal and opposite reaction).
Ask your child to give at least one example of Newton's third law (anything similar to the examples illustrated above).

FOCUS Flight

OBJECTIVE To explore how forces relate to flight

OVERVIEW Nothing moves without some kind of force (push or pull). Flight can happen when the upward push of air is stronger than the downward pull of gravity.

WHAT TO DO

With your team, carefully follow each step below.

Observe

Look at the pictures on page 184. **Observe** how these objects are different from each other. Now **talk** about some things these objects might have in common.

Describe

Describe each object on page 184. What does it **look** like? What **color** is it? What **shape** is it? What is it doing? How **heavy** is it compared to the other objects?

Discuss

What force does a bulldozer use to move dirt? push

What force does a truck use to tow a trailer? pull

What is the "upward push" airplanes use to fly? lift

Flight can happen when the upward push of air is stronger than the downward pull of gravity. Read the story below to find out more.

How Things Fly

Flight depends on the force of air pushing up.

Nothing moves without some kind of force (push or pull). For an object to fly, the upward push of air, called "lift," must be stronger than the downward pull of gravity.

An airplane uses lift.

The shape of the wing creates lift.

Because it is curved, the top of an airplane's wing is longer than the bottom. Air on top must flow faster to go the same distance.

Lift pushes the airplane up.

The slower air under the wing has higher air pressure. This higher pressure pushes the wing upwards. Scientists call this "lift."

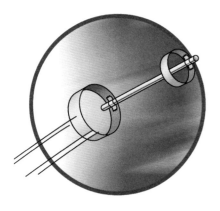

A "flying loop" uses lift.

The shape of the loop creates lift.

A loop is like a kind of wing. Air moves faster over the outside of the top half and the inside of the bottom half creating lift.

Lift pushes the loop up.

Because of its shape, air also goes faster through the loop than it does under it. The slower air under the loop pushes up.

A "flying disc" uses lift.

The shape of the disc creates lift.

The curved upper surface of a disc acts as a kind of wing. The spin of the disc helps keep it stable so lift can push up equally.

Lift pushes the disc up.

Even though wings, loops, and discs are different, they all use shape to create lift to overcome the downward pull of gravity.

WHAT I LEARNED - part 1

Discuss the story with your team, then answer the questions below.

1 How does the shape of a plane's wings affect air flow?

_____

_____

_____

_____

2 How are a loop and a disc similar? How are they different?

_____

_____

_____

_____

3 If a plane's wings were upside down, how would lift change?

_____

_____

_____

_____

DO THE ACTIVITY

Working with your research team, carefully follow each step below. Before you start, be sure you know the **safety rules** for this activity.

STEP 1

Fold one paper strip in half. **Cut** it along the fold line and **discard** half. **Tape** the ends together to make a loop. Now **tape** the long strip to make a second loop.

STEP 2

Tape the loops to the straw as shown. Be sure the ends of the straw are flush with the edges of the loops, and that both loops are straight.

STEP 3

Following directions from your teacher, **throw** the "flying loop." **Measure** how far it goes. **Repeat** until everyone on your team has had a turn.

STEP 4

Review the flights from step 3. **Discuss** your observations with your research team, then **compare** your findings with those of other teams.

WHAT I LEARNED - part 2

Discuss the activity with your team, then answer the questions below.

1 What made your loop fly? (hint: see page 184)

_____

_____

_____

_____

_____

_____

2 How were the step 3 flights similar? How were they different?

_____

_____

_____

_____

_____

_____

_____

3 What might happen if the loops were smashed? Why?

_____

_____

_____

_____

_____

_____

_____

SHOW WHAT YOU KNOW - 1

For something to fly, **lift** must be stronger than **gravity**. Lift is affected by an object's **shape**. Circle the objects below that can fly, then fill in the correct words.

This pulls down:

_____

- - - - - - - - - - - - - - -

This pushes up:

_____

- - - - - - - - - - - - - - -

This can affect lift:

_____

- - - - - - - - - - - - - - -

To the Parent . . .

Scripture Connection: James 4:10

Lesson Focus:
Flight

Lesson Objective:
To explore how forces relate to flight

National Science Education Standards:
Standard B2 — *"All students should develop an understanding of position and motion of objects . . . (both) can be changed by pushing or pulling . . . sound is produced by vibrating objects . . . pitch can be varied by changing rate of vibration . . ."*

Follow-up Questions:
Ask your child what the force of air pushing up on a wing is called (lift).
Ask your child to name one thing that can affect the amount of lift a wing has (shape).
Ask your child to give examples of things that use lift to fly (anything similar to the correct illustrations above).

Simple Machines
Lesson 30

FOCUS Simple Machines

OBJECTIVE To explore how a simple machine can change the direction of a force

OVERVIEW Simple machines (like levers, pulleys, and wheels) can be used to change the direction of a force. We use many kinds of simple machines every day.

WHAT TO DO

With your team, carefully follow each step below.

Observe

Look at the pinwheel, the ruler, the spool, and the dowel. **Think** about the shape of each item. **Talk** about things you might do with each one.

Describe

Describe each item. What does it **look** like? What does it **feel** like? What **color** is it? What **shape** is it? How is it **similar** to or **different** from the other items?

Discuss

What is needed to make anything move? force

What can change direction of a force? machine

What can simple machines help us do? work

Simple machines (like levers, pulleys, and wheels) can be used to change the direction of a force. Read the story below to learn more about simple machines.

Simple Machines

Simple machines can change the direction of force.

Nothing can move without some kind of force. Simple machines can change the direction of a force. This makes many kinds of work much easier to do.

This is a lever.

Push one end down, the other goes up.

When you push down on one end of a lever, the other end goes up. Levers can help raise heavy objects.

There are many kinds of levers.

A paint can opener is a lever. So is a crowbar, the handle of a hammer, and many other tools. Even a seesaw is a lever!

This is a pulley.

Pull one end down, the other goes up.

When you pull down on a rope attached to a pulley, the other end of the rope goes up. Pulleys can help lift heavy loads.

There are many kinds of pulleys.

Flag poles have pulleys to raise and lower flags. There are tiny plastic pulleys in mini-blinds, and huge steel pulleys in cranes.

This is a wheel and axle.

The wheel goes around. The bike moves forward.

The wheels of a moving bicycle turn round and round, pushing backward against the ground. This makes the bike go forward.

There are many kinds of wheels and axles.

Wheels and axles are everywhere — bikes, planes, wagons, trains — even in pizza cutters, doorknobs, and pencil sharpeners!

WHAT I LEARNED - part 1

Discuss the story with your team, then answer the questions below.

1 Name three simple machines. Give an example of each one.

_____

_____

_____

_____

_____

2 How are pulleys and levers similar? How are they different?

_____

_____

_____

_____

_____

_____

3 How might your town be different if there were no wheels?

_____

_____

_____

_____

_____

DO THE ACTIVITY

Working with your research team, carefully follow each step below. Before you start, be sure you know the **safety rules** for this activity.

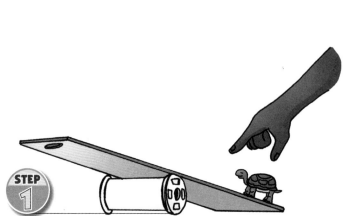

STEP 1

Place the ruler across the spool. **Place** the turtle on the blue dot. Now **observe** the turtle's motion as you slowly **push down** on the red dot. **Record** the results.

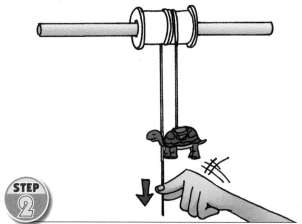

STEP 2

Slip the dowel through the spool. **Wrap** the string around the spool. **Tape** one end to the turtle. **Pull** the other end and **observe** the turtle's motion. **Record** the results.

STEP 3

Hold the pinwheel as shown. **Push** air toward the pinwheel by **blowing** at it softly. **Observe** the motion of the hole as you blow. **Record** the results.

STEP 4

Review each step in this activity. **Discuss** how each machine changed the direction of force. **Compare** your team's findings with other research teams.

WHAT I LEARNED - part 2

Discuss the activity with your team, then answer the questions below.

1 What was the simple machine in step 1? In step 2? In step 3?

_____

_____

_____

_____

_____

_____

2 How are a lever and a seesaw alike? How are they different?

_____

_____

_____

_____

_____

_____

3 How might you use a simple machine to change a force?

_____

_____

_____

_____

_____

_____

SHOW WHAT YOU KNOW - 1

A simple machine (like a **lever**, a **pulley**, or a **wheel** and **axle**) can change the direction of a force. Read each line below, then fill in the name of the simple machine that it describes.

Push one end down. The other goes up.

_____

_____

Pull one end down. The other goes up.

_____

_____

It goes around. Something moves forward.

_____

_____

To the Parent . . .   **Scripture Connection:** 2 Chronicles 26:15

Lesson Focus:
Simple Machines

Lesson Objective:
To explore how simple machines change the direction of a force

National Science Education Standards:
Standard B2 — *"All students should develop an understanding of position and motion of objects . . . (both) can be changed by pushing or pulling . . . sound is produced by vibrating objects . . . pitch can be varied by changing rate of vibration . . ."*

Follow-up Questions:
Ask your child to name three simple machines (lever, pulley, wheel and axle).
Ask your child to give at least one example of a simple machine (seesaw = lever, flagpole = pulley, etc.).
Ask your child to explain how one simple machine changes the direction of a force (pushing down, raises up, etc.).

FOCUS   Refraction

OBJECTIVE   To explore how light is bent by a lens

OVERVIEW   To see anything, we need light. Light usually travels in straight lines. But some things can make light bend (refract). When light refracts, strange things can happen!

WHAT TO DO

With your team, carefully follow each step below.

Observe

Look at the large coin. **Look** at it again through the magnifying lens. How does it look different? **Observe** other coins and small objects using the lens.

Describe

Describe the large coin. What does it **look** like? What does it **feel** like? What **shape** is it? How does it **change** when you look at it through the magnifying lens?

Discuss

What is needed for us to see anything? light

What word can mean "to bend light"? refract

What word can mean "to make larger"? magnify

Light usually travels in a straight line. But some things can make light bend (refract). Read the story below to find out what happens when light bends.

Bending Light

Sometimes light bends. Scientists call this "refraction."

Light usually travels in a straight line. But sometimes light can bend (refract). When light refracts, it can makes objects look different. It can even make colors appear!

Refraction can magnify.

A lens can cause refraction.

The curved surface of a lens causes light passing through it to refract. Objects seen through a lens can look bigger.

Many devices use a lens to magnify.

A camera uses a lens to magnify. So do things like telescopes, microscopes, reading glasses, and binoculars.

Refraction can make illusions.

Water can cause refraction.

If you push a straight stick halfway into a pool of still water, refraction makes it seem to bend where it enters the water.

A mirror can cause refraction.

If a mirror's surface is curved, it causes light to refract. This can make the reflection you see look very strange!

Refraction can make rainbows.

A water drop can cause refraction.

The curved surface of a water drop can bend light, too. When light is bent different amounts, it can make different colors.

Raindrops make rainbows!

If the angle of the sunlight is just right, raindrops refract light into all its basic colors. That's when we see a beautiful rainbow!

WHAT I LEARNED - part 1

Discuss the story with your team, then answer the questions below.

1 What is refraction? Name 3 things refraction can do to light.

_____

_____

_____

_____

_____

_____

2 How are a telescope and microscope alike? How do they differ?

_____

_____

_____

_____

_____

_____

3 Why isn't there a rainbow every time it rains?

_____

_____

_____

_____

_____

DO THE ACTIVITY

Working with your research team, carefully follow each step below. Before you start, be sure you know the **safety rules** for this activity.

STEP 1

Place the large coin on the paper towel. Carefully **observe** its surface. Now **fill** the pipette with water. **Place** one drop of water in the center of the coin.

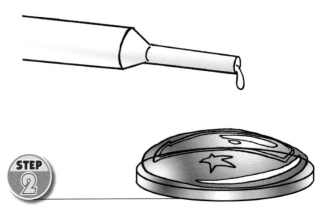

STEP 2

Continue adding drops (one at a time) until the coin is full. Now **look** through the water at the coin's surface. **Compare** this with how it looked in step 1.

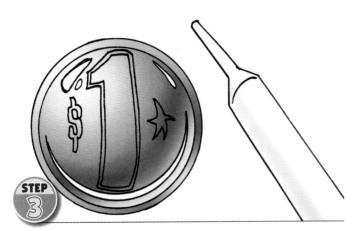

STEP 3

Repeat steps 1 and 2 using both sides of the second coin. **Record** your observations. Make sure that everyone on your team has had a turn.

STEP 4

Review each step in this activity. **Discuss** how the water changed the way the coins looked. **Compare** your team's findings with those of other research teams.

WHAT I LEARNED - part 2

Discuss the activity with your team, then answer the questions below.

1 How did the "bump" of water make the coins look different?

_____

_____

_____

_____

_____

_____

2 How are a water drop and lens alike? How are they different?

_____

_____

_____

_____

_____

_____

3 Which magnifies better, a lens or a water drop? Why?

_____

_____

_____

_____

_____

_____

NAME _____

SHOW WHAT YOU KNOW - 1

Refraction is when light bends. Write the correct word on the line below. Circle any objects that might cause light to refract, changing what we see.

When light bends, it is called

_____

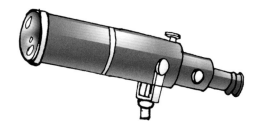

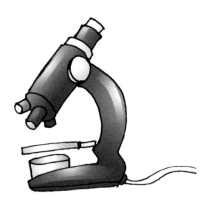

To the Parent . . .   **Scripture Connection:** Genesis 9:13

Lesson Focus:
Refraction

Lesson Objective:
To explore how light is bent by a lens

National Science Education Standards:
Standard B3 — *"All students should develop an understanding of . . . the properties of light, heat, electricity, and magnetism . . . light can be reflected by a mirror, refracted by a lens, or absorbed by the object . . ."*

Follow-up Questions:
Ask your child what "refraction" means (refraction is the scientific term for "bending light").
Ask your child what a lens does, and what most lenses are used for (refracts or bends light; to magnify).
Ask your child for examples of devices with lenses (telescope, microscope, binoculars, reading glasses, etc.).

FOCUS Reflection and Refraction

OBJECTIVE To explore two basic properties of light

OVERVIEW Light usually bounces off things (reflects). But sometimes light also bends (refracts). There are many useful ways to use these special properties of light.

WHAT TO DO

With your team, carefully follow each step below.

Observe

Look at the front of the mirror. **Think** about what you see. Now **look** at the back of the mirror. **How** does this view differ from what you saw in the front of the mirror?

Describe

Describe the mirror. What does it **look** like? What does it **feel** like? What **shape** is it? What **color** is it? How is it like other mirrors that you've seen? How is it different?

Discuss

What do we need in order to see anything? light

What word can mean "to bounce off"? reflect

What word can mean "to bend light"? refract

Light bouncing off something is called **reflection**. Light being bent by something is called **refraction**. Read the story below to discover more about light.

Changing Light
Light changes directions in interesting ways.
Light usually bounces off of things. Scientists call this "reflection." Light can also be bent by certain things. Scientists call the bending of light "refraction."

Light can reflect.
We need reflection to see.
To see anything, we need light. Unless it gives off light itself, an object can only be seen because of the light it reflects.

Reflection can bounce back images.
Mirrors are great reflectors. They reflect the light shining on things. Mirror images are usually right-side up, but reversed!

Light can refract.
Refraction can create illusions.
Refraction makes light change its path. If you place a pencil in water, refraction can make the pencil look broken or bent!

Refraction can make rainbows.
The curved surface of raindrops can bend light. If the angle of sunlight is just right, raindrops refract light into its basic colors.

Light is used in many ways.
Reflection can be helpful.
The most common "reflectors" are mirrors. They are used for everything from combing hair, to driving a car, to fixing teeth!

Refraction can be helpful.
The most common "refractors" are lenses. Lenses are used in devices like cameras, telescopes, lasers, and microscopes.

WHAT I LEARNED - part 1

Discuss the story with your team, then answer the questions below.

1 What are some ways we can use reflection and refraction?

_____

_____

_____

_____

2 Explain how reflection and refraction are different.

_____

_____

_____

_____

3 Do you usually see rainbows at night? Why or why not?

_____

_____

_____

_____

DO THE ACTIVITY

Working with your research team, carefully follow each step below. Before you start, be sure you know the **safety rules** for this activity.

STEP 1

Place the mirror in the jar so that the glass side is facing you and the top is tilted back. **Look** into the mirror from table level and **describe** what you see.

STEP 2

Shine the flashlight directly at the mirror (touching the jar). **Look** up and **observe** the ceiling. **Move** the flashlight around to vary the reflected light.

STEP 3

Fill the jar with water. **Repeat** step 2. Look at the ceiling and **observe** how the "refracted" light differs from the "reflected" light that you saw in step 2.

STEP 4

Review each step in this activity. **Discuss** how the light changed in steps 2 and 3. **Compare** your team's findings with those of other research teams.

WHAT I LEARNED - part 2

Discuss the activity with your team, then answer the questions below.

1 Where did the beam of light begin? Where did it end?

_____

_____

_____

_____

_____

_____

2 How were steps 2 and 3 alike? How were they different?

_____

_____

_____

_____

_____

_____

3 How might a brighter flashlight change the rainbow? Why?

_____

_____

_____

_____

_____

_____

SHOW WHAT YOU KNOW - 1

Light can be **reflected** or **refracted**. Write the correct word on the lines below. Circle in red pictures that show reflection. Circle in blue pictures that show refraction.

When light "bounces off," it is

_____

_____

When light "bends," it is

_____

_____

To the Parent . . .   **Scripture Connection:** Colossians 3:9-10

Lesson Focus:
Reflection / Refraction

Lesson Objective:
To explore two common properties of light

National Science Education Standards:
Standard B3 — *"All students should develop an understanding of . . . the properties of light, heat, electricity, and magnetism . . . light can be reflected by a mirror, refracted by a lens, or absorbed by the object . . ."*

Follow-up Questions:
Ask your child what "reflection" means (reflection is the scientific term for when light "bounces off" an object).
Ask your child what "refraction" means (refraction is the scientific term for when light is "bent" by something).
Ask your child to name a device that uses a lens to refract light (telescope, microscope, camera, etc.).

Finding Friction
Lesson 33

FOCUS Friction

OBJECTIVE To explore some of the characteristics of friction

OVERVIEW Friction can produce heat or slow moving things down. Rough surfaces usually cause more friction. Reducing friction usually makes things easier to move.

WHAT TO DO

With your team, carefully follow each step below.

Observe

Look at the sandpaper. **Look** at the wheels on the car. **Rub** your finger on the sandpaper. Now spin one of the car's wheels. **Think** about how the friction felt different.

Describe

Describe the sandpaper and the car wheels. What do they **look** like? What do they **feel** like? **Describe** how it feels to slide your finger along each one.

Discuss

What does rubbing things together cause? friction

What is one thing that friction can produce? heat

What type of surface causes more friction? rough

Usually the more friction there is between two objects, the hotter they get, and the more they will slow down. Read the story below to find out more.

Friction

Friction happens all around us!

Friction occurs whenever two objects rub together, or when an object rubs against some other surface. Friction can be harmful or helpful depending on the situation.

Friction can be harmful.

Friction takes energy.

Friction slows everything down. To overcome friction when riding a bike, you must apply energy by pedaling harder.

Friction produces heat.

Energy lost to friction can turn to heat. Too much heat can be harmful. For instance, sliding against carpet may "burn" you.

Friction can be helpful.

Friction helps us move.

If you've ever tried to walk on ice, you know too little friction can be a problem! It takes some friction just to move around.

Friction keeps thing in place.

Friction also helps keep things from moving. For instance, a little friction can keep your glasses from sliding off your nose!

Friction can be changed.

Friction can be reduced.

Lubricants (like oil) help reduce friction in machines. Wheels or rollers also help reduce friction, making things easier to move.

Friction can be increased.

Special materials and special shapes can increase friction. Look at the bottom of shoes or at different kinds of car tires.

WHAT I LEARNED - part 1

Discuss the story with your team, then answer the questions below.

1 Name at least two different ways friction can be changed.

_____

_____

_____

_____

_____

2 How can friction be harmful? How can friction be helpful?

_____

_____

_____

_____

_____

_____

_____

3 Which is harder to walk through — tall grass or short? Why?

_____

_____

_____

_____

DO THE ACTIVITY

Working with your research team, carefully follow each step below. Before you start, be sure you know the **safety rules** for this activity.

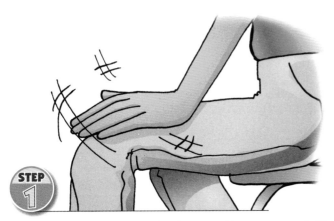

STEP 1

Rub your hands together rapidly. **Discuss** how they feel. **Rub** one hand against your leg rapidly. **Discuss** how this feels. Why did the temperature change?

STEP 2

Make a ramp from two hard-back books (see illustration). **Place** the car at the top of the ramp. **Release** the car. **Observe** and **record** the results.

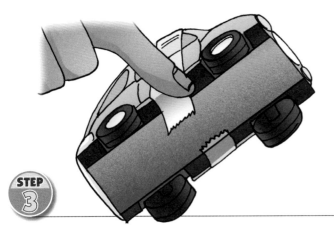

STEP 3

Tape a strip of sandpaper to the bottom of the car. (Make sure it is rough side down and will touch the ramp.) Now **repeat** step 2 using the modified car.

STEP 4

Review steps 2 and 3. **Discuss** how added friction changed the way the car performed. **Compare** your findings with those of other research teams.

WHAT I LEARNED - part 2

Discuss the activity with your team, then answer the questions below.

1 Describe two things that friction can do.

_____

_____

_____

_____

_____

_____

2 How were steps 2 and 3 similar? How were they different?

_____

_____

_____

_____

_____

_____

3 Which surface might create more friction — ice or sand? Why?

_____

_____

_____

_____

_____

_____

NAME _____

SHOW WHAT YOU KNOW - 1

More friction can produce heat or minimize slipping. **Less** friction can make moving easier. Write the correct word in the lines below. Circle ways to *increase* friction in red. Circle ways to *reduce* friction in blue.

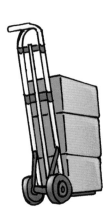

_____ friction produces heat.

_____ friction causes slipping.

To the Parent . . .   **Scripture Connection:** Ephesians 4:26

Lesson Focus:
Friction

Lesson Objective:
To explore some of the characteristics of friction

National Science Education Standards:
Standard B3 — *"All students should develop an understanding of . . . the properties of light, heat, electricity, and magnetism . . . heat can be produced in many ways such as burning, rubbing* (friction), *or mixing substances . . . "*

Follow-up Questions:
Ask your child what friction usually creates. Ask for an example (heat; rubbing hands together, getting "carpet burn," etc.).
Ask your child to describe some ways to reduce friction (lubricants like oil; wheels, rollers, etc.).
Ask your child to describe some ways to increase friction (special materials and shapes, as in sneaker soles, tire treads, etc.).

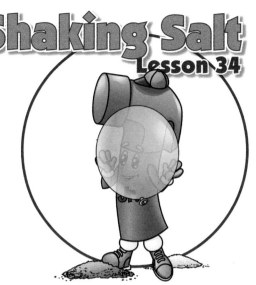

FOCUS Static Electricity

OBJECTIVE To explore the relationship between atoms and static electricity

OVERVIEW Everything is made of atoms. Atoms have "positive" and "negative" particles. When these particles give atoms different "charges," the atoms can cause static electricity.

WHAT TO DO

With your team, carefully follow each step below.

Observe

Look at the salt. **Look** at the sawdust. **Observe** the size of the pieces. **Look** at the balloon. **Compare** the way it feels to the feel of the salt and the sawdust.

Describe

Describe the salt. What does it **look** like? What does it **feel** like? What does it **smell** like? What **shape** is it? How is it similar to sawdust? How is it different?

Discuss

What is everything on Earth made from? atoms

What is one thing an atom can have? charge

What is one simple form of electricity? static

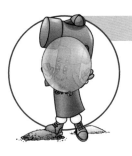

Everything is made of atoms. Atoms with different "charges" can cause static electricity. Read the story below to find out more.

Static Electricity

Atoms can cause static electricity.

Everything is made of atoms. Atoms have "positive" and "negative" particles. When these particles give atoms different "charges," the atoms can cause static electricity.

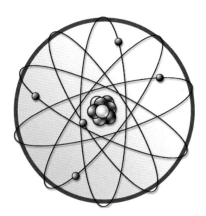

This is an atom.

Everything is made of atoms.

Atoms are tiny particles of matter that are far too small to see. Everything on Earth is made from a combination of atoms.

Atoms are made from tiny parts.

The atom's center is tightly-packed "protons" and "neutrons." They are surrounded by fast-moving particles called "electrons."

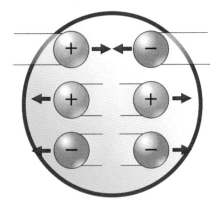

Atoms can be "charged."

Atoms can be positive or negative.

Atoms with fewer electrons have a "positive" (+) charge. Atoms with more electrons have a "negative" (-) charge.

Charges can attract or repel.

Atoms with opposite charges (+ -) pull toward each other. Atoms with the same charge (+ + or - -) move away from each other.

Charges make static electricity.

Electrons try to balance opposite charges.

Static electricity happens when the positive and negative charges of atoms are not equal. Electrons try to move to restore balance. They may even jump from one object to another.

Walk across thick carpet and you pick up electrons. To restore balance, they may jump from your hand to a doorknob. Ouch!

WHAT I LEARNED - part 1

Discuss the story with your team, then answer the questions below.

1 What are atoms? Why are atoms important?

_____

_____

_____

_____

_____

_____

2 How are positive and negative atoms different from each other?

_____

_____

_____

_____

_____

_____

3 If charges are equal, is there more static electricity or less? Why?

_____

_____

_____

_____

_____

DO THE ACTIVITY

Working with your research team, carefully follow each step below. Before you start, be sure you know the **safety rules** for this activity.

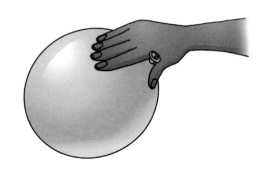

STEP 1

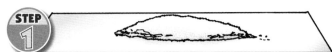

Pour a small pile of salt on the desktop. **Inflate** a balloon and tie it off. **Move** the balloon just above the salt and **observe** what happens.

STEP 2

Have a team member "charge" the balloon by **rubbing** it on his/her hair for 30 seconds. Quickly **move** the balloon just above the salt and **observe** what happens.

STEP 3

Compare what happened in steps 1 and 2 and record your observations. Now **repeat** step 2 using a pile of sawdust instead. **Record** the results.

STEP 4

Review each step. **Discuss** what you did to change how the salt and sawdust reacted. **Compare** your findings with those of other research teams.

WHAT I LEARNED - part 2

Discuss the activity with your team, then answer the questions below.

1 What did your team do to "charge" the balloon?

_____

_____

_____

_____

_____

_____

2 How are salt and sawdust alike? How are they different?

_____

_____

_____

_____

_____

_____

3 How might a charged balloon affect dust particles? Why?

_____

_____

_____

_____

_____

_____

SHOW WHAT YOU KNOW - 1

When atoms do not have the same "charge," they can cause static electricity. Circle the objects that show static electricity, then complete the sentence below.

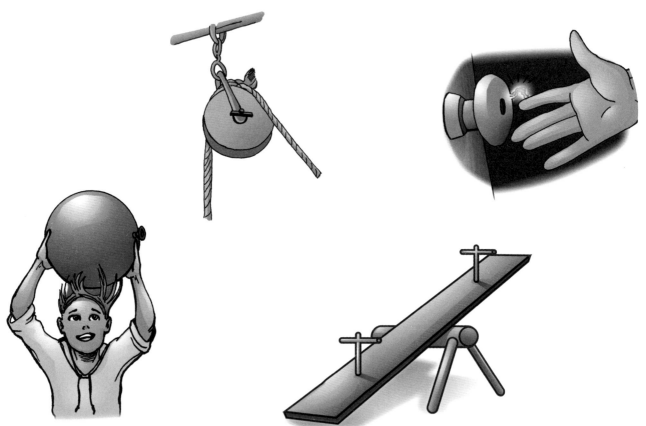

When electrons in atoms try to restore balance, they can cause

_____

_____

To the Parent . . .   **Scripture Connection:** Colossians 1:17

Lesson Focus:
Static Electricity

Lesson Objective:
To explore the relationship between atoms and static electricity

National Science Education Standards:
Standard B3 — *"All students should develop an understanding of . . . the properties of light, heat, electricity, and magnetism . . . atoms have measurable properties such as mass and electrical charge . . ."*

Follow-up Questions:
Ask your child what all matter is made from (atoms).
Ask your child what gives an atom a negative or positive charge (more or fewer electrons).
Ask your child why electrons sometimes cause a "spark" of static electricity (they are trying to move to restore balance).

FOCUS Magnetism

OBJECTIVE To explore some properties of magnets and magnetism

OVERVIEW All materials have characteristics called "properties." Magnets have a property called magnetism. Magnetism affects how magnets relate to each other and to other materials.

Attracting Iron
Lesson 35

WHAT TO DO

With your team, carefully follow each step below.

Observe

Look at the magnets. **Look** at the iron filings. **Look** at the sawdust. **Think** about ways these items are similar. **Think** about ways they are different.

Describe

Describe the iron filings. What do they **look** like? What do they **feel** like? What **color** are they? How do the iron filings compare to the sawdust?

Discuss

What's another name for characteristic? property

What property do magnets have? magnetism

What is one thing magnets can do? attract

Magnets have a characteristic called **magnetism**. This affects how magnets react to each other and to other materials. Read the story below to find out more.

Magnetism

Magnets have "magnetism."

All magnets have a characteristic called "magnetism." Magnetism affects how these magnets react to each other. It also controls how they react to other materials.

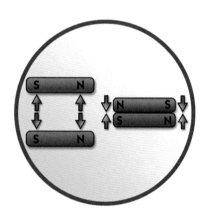

These are magnets.

Magnets can attract.

Magnets have a north pole and a south pole. If you place opposite poles near each other, the magnets will pull together.

Magnets can also repel.

If you place poles that are the same together, the magnets will push apart. They will turn so opposite poles are touching.

These are iron bolts.

Iron is "magnetic."

Iron is called "magnetic" because magnets stick to it. (A note magnet stuck to a refrigerator is a good example.)

Few materials are magnetic.

Although some common metals are magnetic (iron, cobalt, nickel), many other metals (like copper and aluminum) are not.

These are wood chips.

Wood is "non-magnetic."

Wood is a "non-magnetic" material because it is not attracted by magnets. A magnet will not stick to a wooden door.

Most materials are non-magnetic.

Materials like glass, plastic, and paper are non-magnetic. To test any material for magnetism, simply touch it with a magnet.

WHAT I LEARNED - part 1

Discuss the story with your team, then answer the questions below.

1 What do "like" poles do? What do "opposite" poles do?

_____

_____

_____

_____

2 How are iron bolts and wood chips different from each other?

_____

_____

_____

_____

3 How could a magnet help separate nails from sawdust?

_____

_____

_____

_____

DO THE ACTIVITY

Working with your research team, carefully follow each step below. Before you start, be sure you know the **safety rules** for this activity.

STEP 1

Pour a spoonful of iron filings into each plastic bag. **Seal** the bags carefully. **Hold** one bag by the top and **move** a magnet close to it. **Record** the results.

STEP 2

Stick the magnet to the bag. **Add** the other bag to make a "magnet sandwich." **Record** the results. Now **remove** the magnet and **observe** what happens.

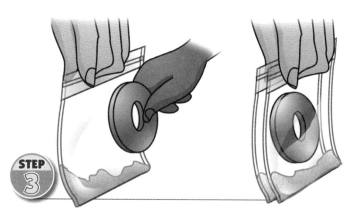

STEP 3

Pour the iron filings back into their bottle. **Repeat** steps 1 and 2 using sawdust instead of iron filings. **Record** the results. **Pour** the sawdust back into its bag.

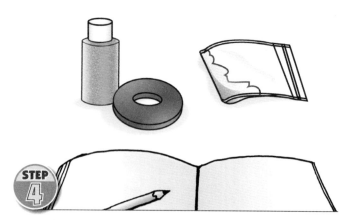

STEP 4

Review each step in this activity. **Discuss** how the materials reacted to the magnet. **Compare** your team's findings with those of other teams.

WHAT I LEARNED - part 2

Discuss the activity with your team, then answer the questions below.

1 What effect did the magnet have on the two materials?

_____

_____

_____

_____

2 How were the filings and sawdust alike? How did they differ?

_____

_____

_____

_____

3 What effect might a magnet have on an iron pan? Why?

_____

_____

_____

_____

WHAT I LEARNED - part 2

SHOW WHAT YOU KNOW - 1

A magnet's poles can **attract** or **repel**. Write the correct word on the lines below. Circle "magnetic" materials in red. Circle "non-magnetic" materials in blue.

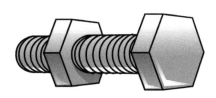

What do "opposite" poles do?

_____

_ _ _ _ _ _ _ _ _ _ _ _ _ _

_____

What do "like" poles do?

_____

_ _ _ _ _ _ _ _ _ _ _ _ _ _

_____

| **To the Parent . . .** | **Scripture Connection:** Hebrews 4:16 |

Lesson Focus:
Magnetism

Lesson Objective:
To explore some properties of magnets and magnetism

National Science Education Standards:
Standard B3 — *"All students should develop an understanding of . . . the properties of light, heat, electricity, and magnetism . . . magnets attract and repel each other and certain kinds of other materials . . ."*

Follow-up Questions:
Ask your child what happens when you move "opposite" poles of magnets toward each other (they pull together, attract).
Ask your child what happens when you move "like" poles of magnets toward each other (they push apart, repel).
Ask your child to give some examples of magnetic and non-magnetic materials (answers will vary).

Managing Magnetism
Lesson 36

FOCUS   Magnetism

OBJECTIVE   To explore some practical applications of magnetism

OVERVIEW   Knowing magnets are attracted to certain metals is "science." Applying that knowledge to sort trash, lock doors, or run electric motors is "technology."

WHAT TO DO

With your team, carefully follow each step below.

Observe

Look at the iron filings. **Look** at the sawdust. **Look** at the salt. **Think** about some ways these items are similar. **Think** about some ways they are different.

Describe

Describe each of the materials you observed. What do they **look** like? What do they **feel** like? What are some places you might find materials like these?

Discuss

What is one thing magnets usually attract? metal

What is knowing about materials called? science

What is applying science called? technology

Understanding **magnetism** helps us use magnets for many useful tasks. In our modern world, magnets are all around us! Read the story below to find out more.

Managing Magnetism

Magnetism has many uses.

Magnetism is a word that describes how magnets react to each other and to other materials. Understanding how magnetism works helps us perform many useful tasks.

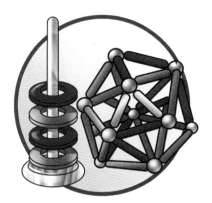

Magnets are used at home.

Magnets can hold things.

Magnets can hold notes on a refrigerator or paper clips in a cup. Some shower curtains use magnets to hold the bottom in place.

Magnets can make interesting toys.

Some magnetic toys seem to float. Others make unusual shapes. Some use magnets to fasten wooden train cars together.

Magnets are used on farms.

Magnets can help clean.

Some farmers use large magnets on wheels to pick up loose metal (like nails and screws) from driveways, shops, and barns.

Magnets can help protect cows.

Cow magnets are put into some cows' stomachs. They can safely hold any metal bits the cow might accidently eat.

Magnets are used in industry.

Magnets can help sort trash.

Recyclers use huge magnets to separate magnetic materials (like steel) from non-magnetic materials (like plastic and paper).

Magnets are in electric motors.

Magnets help drive electric motors — from tiny fans to giant generators. Without magnets, we would have no electricity!

Discuss the story with your team, then answer the questions below.

1 Name at least three different ways people use magnets.

_____

_____

_____

_____

_____

_____

2 Name three different kinds of magnets and tell how they differ.

_____

_____

_____

_____

_____

_____

3 How might your life change if there were no magnets?

_____

_____

_____

_____

_____

_____

DO THE ACTIVITY

Working with your research team, carefully follow each step below. Before you start, be sure you know the **safety rules** for this activity.

STEP 1

Pour the iron filings, salt, and sawdust into the petri dish. **Stir** them together with the craft stick. **Discuss** ways you might separate these materials.

STEP 2

Place the magnet in the bag. Slowly **drag** the bag across the mixture of iron filings, salt, and sawdust in the petri dish. **Record** the result.

STEP 3

Continue dragging the bag back and forth through the pile until one material is completely removed. **Discuss** how you used "technology" to sort materials.

STEP 4

Review each step. **Discuss** how each material reacted to the magnet. What "science" was used? **Compare** your findings with those of other teams.

WHAT I LEARNED - part 2

Discuss the activity with your team, then answer the questions below.

1 What effect did the magnet have on each material?

_____

_____

_____

_____

_____

_____

2 How were the materials similar? How were they different?

_____

_____

_____

_____

_____

_____

3 Why can huge magnets be used to help sort piles of trash?

_____

_____

_____

_____

_____

_____

SHOW WHAT YOU KNOW - 1

Magnets are all around us. Magnetic **technology** helps us perform many useful tasks. Circle objects with magnets in red. Circle objects without magnets in blue.

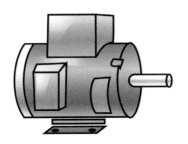

Using a science like magnetism to perform practical tasks is called

_____

To the Parent . . .   **Scripture Connection:** 2 Timothy 3:14

Lesson Focus:
Magnetism

Lesson Objective:
To explore some practical applications (technology) of magnetism

National Science Education Standards:
Standard B3 — *"All students should develop an understanding of . . . the properties of light, heat, electricity, and magnetism . . . magnets attract and repel each other and certain kinds of other materials . . ."*

Follow-up Questions:
Ask your child to describe some ways magnets are used at home (refrigerator magnets, shower curtain magnets, toys, etc.).
Ask your child to describe some ways magnets are used on farms and in industry (cow magnets, power generation, etc.).
Ask your child why there would be no electricity without magnets (electric motors and generators need magnets to work).

Appendix

Mercury

Venus

Earth

Mars

Jupiter

Saturn

Uranus

Neptune

Pluto

Sun